Creative
Crochet
Handbook

Creative Crochet Handbook

CHRISTA PALFY

ANGUS & ROBERTSON PUBLISHERS

Angus & Robertson

London . Sydney . Melbourne . Singapore

Manila

This book is copyright. Apart from any fair dealing for
the purposes of private study, research, criticism or
review, as permitted under the Copyright Act, no part
may be reproduced by any process without written permission.
Inquiries should be addressed to the publishers.

First published by Angus & Robertson Publishers, Australia, 1977
Reprinted 1978

© Christa Palfy 1976

National Library of Australia
card number and ISBN 0 207 13282 8

Printed in Hong Kong

CONTENTS

PART I Common Crochet

PART II Tricot

PART III Lace Tricot

FOREWORD

This book introduces the beginner to the art of crochet, a handcraft that is daily gaining in popularity; but it is also intended for the more advanced crocheter, who will find in it many exciting and refreshingly new ideas.

Many of the stitch and pattern exercises are based on those used in my handcraft classes. They have been adapted to suit readers who want to learn without outside help. At the same time the exercises are arranged in a form that is suitable for class teaching.

Three types of crocheting are explained in detail, illustrated with exercises ranging from simple stitches to the making of garments and other articles.

Common crochet, the best known form of the art, is the subject of the first part of the book. In the second part I have introduced new and hitherto unpublished stitches and patterns for Tunisian or Afghan crocheting, also known as tricot, as well as describing and illustrating the more familiar Tunisian stitches and patterns. I hope this will result in a revival of interest in this delightful form of crochet.

The third part of the book is devoted to Lace Tricot, an entirely new method of working with yarn to produce non-stretch textures in a variety of patterns.

For both class teaching and individual learning I recommend for practice the use of a thick brightly coloured wool which does not split. A 12 ply crepe wool and a 4.50 hook (previously no. 7) are suggested: you will find that the stitches show up very clearly and will quickly recognise the differences in their formation.

Beginners are advised to practise the common crochet techniques until thoroughly familiar with them before going on to the tricot and Lace Tricot sections.

Advanced crocheters will still find fresh ideas and new stitch combinations in the first section before working through the parts on tricot and Lace Tricot. Even if you can do tricot and are interested mainly in the new Lace Tricot patterns, you wil find the tricot section worthwhile: there are many helpful hints and ideas, and improvements have been introduced.

I hope crocheting will be as much fun for you as it has always been for me, and that you will enjoy making the garments and other articles in this book as well as inventing your own combinations of stitches and patterns.

I wish to express my thanks to the designers and teachers who have helped me with advice, designs and the checking of the manuscript: special thanks go to Mrs Elaine Wilmot, Mrs Thelma Seckold and Mrs Helen Freeze. I am also indebted to my husband for his valuable time, assistance and patience (and occasional impatience); without him this book could never have been completed.

Christa Palfy

CROCHET HOOK SIZES

International Standard sizes	Old "Wool" sizes	Old "Cotton" sizes
7.00	2	-
6.00	4	-
5.50	5	-
5.00	6	-
4.50	7	-
4.00	8	-
3.50	9	-
3.00	10	3/0
2.50	12	0
2.00	14	1½
1.50	16	3½
1.00	-	5½

BASIC STITCHES
IN COMMON CROCHETING
AND THEIR ABBREVIATIONS

English and Australian usage	U.S. equivalent
chain or chain stitch (ch)	same
double crochet (d c, dc)	single crochet (s c, sc)
slip stitch (sl st, s s, ss)	same
half treble (h tr, htr)	half double crochet (h d c, h dc)
treble (tr)	double crochet (d c, db c, dc)
double treble (d tr, db tr, dbl tr, dtr)	treble (tr)
triple treble (t tr, tr tr, ttr)	double treble (d tr, db tr, dbl tr)

Note: The abbreviations are sometimes used with the full stop; and the same form is often used for both the singular and the plural.

PART I

Common Crochet

INTRODUCTION

Common crochet, the simplest and best-known form of crochet, is amazingly simple — it all begins with a slip loop, just as in knitting. The stitches are worked pulling one loop through another and, however complicated stitches or patterns may appear, they are simply variations on this method. The original loop always remains on the hook once the stitch has been completed and is never counted as a stitch. Once the crochet is finished this last loop is fastened off by cutting or breaking the yarn, drawing it through the last loop, then pulling this end up tightly.

In this section I've given step-by-step instructions to teach the beginner how to work the basic stitches of common crochet and also to refresh the experienced crocheter before moving on to the more complex, but easily mastered, techniques of tricot (also known as Tunisian or Afghan crocheting) and my own invention — Lace Tricot. Lace Tricot is an entirely new method of working with yarn which is ideal for garments as it creates non-stretch textures in a variety of patterns.

Pattern exercises are given at intervals in the step-by-step instructions so that you can consolidate what you've learnt along the way. There are also chapters on particular techniques, for example, two methods to use for finishing off edges. The chapters on understanding abbreviations and reading patterns teach the shorthand language of crochet so that patterns, both in this book and in magazines and booklets, can be easily understood.

The patterns in this section include a multi-coloured cushion cover, a lace stitch stole, an Afghan rug and a treble stitch scarf — all of which can be created using the stitches described here in detail.

HOW TO BEGIN

Step 1
Holding the end of the yarn between the thumb and index finger of the right hand, first place the yarn across the base of the fingers of the left hand (palm facing upwards), then bring it under the index finger.

Step 2
Now bring yarn forward over the left index finger and hold it with the tips of the middle finger and thumb.

Step 3
Hold the hook in the right hand like a pencil.

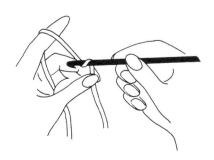

(a) and (b)
Take the hook under and over yarn.

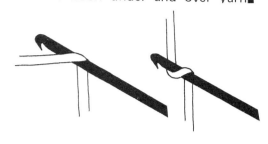

(c)
and twist it right round.

(d)
Then hold the yarn under the loop at the twist, take hook under and over the yarn and draw it through the loop on the hook.

(e)
Tighten the slip knot below the stitch by drawing upwards.

Hold this knot between thumb and middle finger and start your chain, adjusting the tension by passing the yarn round the little finger.

CHAIN STITCH (ch)

This forms the basis of all crochet stitches. Each chain stitch should slip easily over the hook and there should be uniformity of tension right along the chain, for it is the foundation of the whole piece of work.

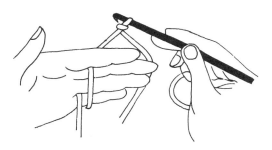

With the first loop on the hook, take the hook under and over the extended yarn. Draw this yarn through the loop on the hook, forming your first chain stitch.

Continue working chain stitches, practising them until they are perfect. Use either the index finger or the little finger of the left hand to adjust the tension, looping the yarn round the index finger once or twice.

TENSION (stitch gauge)

The tension, or the given width of a number of stitches and rows, is very important in the working of garments, as it may vary with individual crocheters. The right tension may be obtained by using a suitable size hook; according to the individual, this may be either smaller or larger than the actual recommended hook size in a particular set of instructions.

BASIC STITCHES

DOUBLE CROCHET

Make 30 chain (a length of 30 chain stitches).

Row 1 Insert hook into second chain (do not count the loop on hook as a chain). Take hook under and over yarn (from now on simply referred to as "yarn over hook" and draw the yarn through the chain.

Yarn over hook, draw through the two loops on the hook. You have now made one double crochet stitch.

Work one double crochet into every chain to the end of row. Turn the work so that the reverse side is facing you for the next row.

Row 2 Work one chain (the "turning chain"), then insert hook under the top two threads of the first stitch (i.e., the last double crochet worked in the previous row),
yarn over hook and draw through (2 threads on hook), yarn over hook

and draw through the 2 loops (one loop remains on hook).
Next double crochet: *insert hook into the top 2 threads of the next double crochet, yarn over hook and draw through, yarn over hook and draw through 2 loops**. Repeat from * to ** to the end of row.

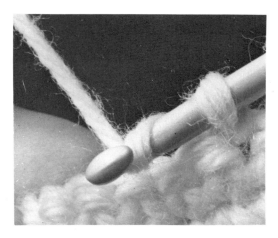

Rows 3 to 8 Work as row 2.

Fasten off by cutting the yarn about 10 cm (4 in) from the work, threading it through the one remaining loop on hook and pulling it tightly. To finish off, thread it neatly into the back of the work, using a wool sewing needle.

HALF TREBLE (htr)

Make 26 chain.

Row 1 Yarn over hook, insert hook under the top thread of the third chain, yarn over hook and draw through chain (3 loops on hook),

yarn over hook and draw through

the 3 loops on hook (1 loop remains on hook).

One half treble is now completed.

Next half treble: *yarn over hook, insert hook under the top thread of the next chain, yarn over hook and draw through chain, yarn over hook and draw through the 3 loops on the hook.**
Work half trebles into every chain to the end of the row, as from * to **.

Row 2 Having turned the work so that the reverse side is facing you, make 2 chain. Do not count these as the first stitches of this row. (Notice when working rows of half treble that there is an extra loop on the wrong side directly below the top two threads of each stitch. Work only into these top two threads.)

Yarn over hook, insert hook under the top 2 threads of the first stitch (the last half treble in the previous row), yarn over hook and draw through same, yarn over hook and draw through the 3 loops on hook, *yarn over hook, insert hook under the top 2 threads of the next half treble, yarn over hook and draw through same, yarn over hook and draw through 3 loops on hook.**

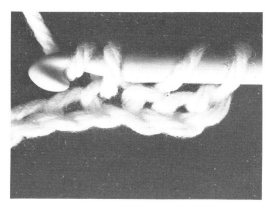

yarn over hook and draw through 2 loops (2 loops left on hook),

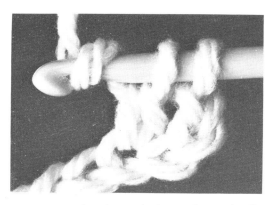

yarn over hook and draw through the remaining 2 loops (1 loop left on hook).**

Repeat from * to ** into every half treble to the end.
Rows 3 to 6 Work as row 2.

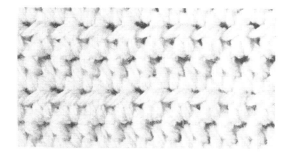

TREBLE STITCH (tr)
Make 30 chain.
Row 1 Yarn over hook, insert hook under the top thread of the fourth chain, *yarn over hook and draw through chain (3 loops on hook),

You have now completed the first treble.

Next treble: yarn over hook, insert hook under top thread of the next chain, repeat from * to **. Work 1 treble into every chain to the end of the row.

Row 2 3 turning chain, yarn over hook, insert hook under top 2 threads of second last treble of previous row *yarn over hook and draw through (3 loops on hook),

yarn over hook and draw through 2 loops (2 loops left on hook), yarn over hook and draw through the remaining 2 loops (1 loop left on hook), **insert hook into top 2 threads of next treble, work next treble as from * to **.

Work 1 treble into every treble to the end of the row, last treble into the upper turning chain.

Rows 3 to 6 Work as row 2.

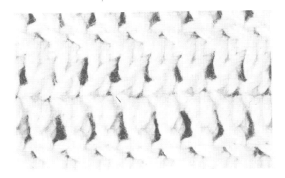

THE TURNING CHAIN

You will have noticed that a certain number of chain stitches are added at the beginning of each row after the work is turned and the reverse side is facing the crocheter. The number of turning chain (chain stitches) needed depends on the stitch that commences the following

9

row.

1 turning chain is needed when the following row is *double crochet*

2 turning chain for *half treble*

3 turning chain for *treble*

4 turning chain for *double treble*

5 turning chain for *triple treble*

For treble, double treble and triple treble this turning chain also stands as the first stitch of the row (this does not apply however to double crochet or half treble). The next treble (or double treble or triple treble) following the turning chain is worked into the second last treble (or double treble or triple treble) of the previous row. The last treble (or double treble or triple treble) in the row is worked into the top or upper turning chain.

POTHOLDER IN TREBLE STITCH
Utilising what we have learned, let's proceed and make a small article.

Materials
1 ball (25 g/1 oz) 8 ply yarn main colour *(A)*.
1 ball (25 g/1 oz) 8 ply yarn contrasting colour *(B)*.
Hook no. 4.00 (no. 8)
Make 42 chain *A*.

Rows 1 to 4 Using *A* work in treble stitch.

Rows 5 and 6 Work *B* in treble stitch (join the different coloured yarns with a reef knot).

Rows 7 to 18 Work in treble stitch, alternating 2 rows of *A* with 2 rows of *B*, the last 2 rows being in *B*.

To make up
Fold in half and sew seams together, matching the stripes. Work 1 row of double crochet in *B* round the top edge of potholder; using *B* make a loop of 12 chain on one corner and work a row of double crochet round the loop, forming a firm hanger. Work in the loose ends of the knots neatly using a wool needle.

DOUBLE TREBLE (dtr)
Make 30 chain.

Row 1 Yarn over hook twice, insert hook into 5th chain, yarn over hook and draw through chain (4 loops on hook),

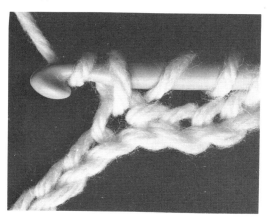

yarn over hook and draw through 2 loops,
yarn over hook and draw through 2 loops again,

yarn over hook and draw through the last 2 loops on hook (1 loop left on hook).

The first double treble is now completed.
Work 1 double treble into every chain to end of row.

Row 2 4 chain, yarn over hook twice, insert hook under top 2 threads of 2nd last double treble in previous row, yarn over hook and draw through (4 loops on hook),

(yarn over hook and draw through 2 loops) 3 times, thus completing your stitch as in row 1.

Work double treble into every double treble of the row to the end, the last double treble being worked into the upper turning chain.

Rows 3 to 6 Work as row 2.

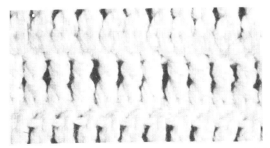

TRIPLE TREBLE (ttr)

Make 30 chain.

Row 1 Yarn over hook 3 times, insert hook into 6th chain, yarn over hook and draw through chain (5 loops on hook),

(yarn over hook and draw through 2 loops) 4 times (1 loop left on hook). This completes 1 triple treble. Work 1 triple treble into every chain to end, turn.

Row 2 5 chain, yarn over hook 3 times, insert hook under the top 2 threads of 2nd last triple treble in previous row (yarn over hook and draw through 2 loops) 4 times (1 loop left on hook).

Work 1 triple treble into every stitch to the end of row, the last triple treble being worked into the upper turning chain.
Rows 3 to 6 Work as row 2.

SLIP STITCH (sl st)
This stitch, sometimes called single crochet, is used when no depth is required — as for the shaping of armholes or for casting off stitches. It is an excellent joining stitch. Firm edges needed for belts, handles of shopping bags and button-band edgings for cardigans and jackets can be obtained by working slip stitch into the top 2 threads of every stitch of the outer row.

The working of slip stitch
Having 1 loop on the hook, insert hook into the next stitch, yarn over hook and draw through the stitch and through loop on hook.

After working the last slip stitch break yarn off, yarn over hook and pull it through the loop tightly.

A practical hint for improved edges
For more advanced crocheters I recommend another method of turning, in place of the commonly used one described earlier. This second technique will improve the edge and will prevent holes from appearing on the side seams of a garment after the pieces are sewn together. Not only the side seams but also the decreased edges, such as those of armholes, will be neater.

This technique may be used for treble, double treble and for triple treble textures; for fancy patterns the common method should be used.

For treble

Turn with 2 chain: 1 treble should replace the 3rd chain of the common turning method and be worked into the treble last worked in the previous

row. Do not count chain as treble. Imagine that your turning chain form a ladder enabling you to climb the correct height of the stitches. The first worked treble counts as the first treble of the next row.

The last treble in row should always be worked into the 2 upper loops between the last treble and the turning chain.

Other trebles

The same method applies to double treble using 3 chain for turning and for triple treble using 4 chain for turning.

If the above instructions are carefully followed you will avoid any mistake in the number of trebles and you will have straight edges.

ABBREVIATIONS

From now on the shorthand language of crochet will be used in the exercises.

The abbreviations for the basic stitches have already been introduced; the list below comprises the more common abbreviations used in the patterns.

A few more abbreviations will be introduced later with the more advanced designs. The crochet instructions in magazines and booklets usually list the abbreviations and the working of the basic stitches before or after the description of the designs.

Abbreviations used stand for both the singular and plural forms; in other words "st" may mean either "stitch" or "stitches".

Watch for the asterisks (*), as these and sometimes the brackets ( ) signify the beginning and the end of steps which are to be repeated later in the instructions. More about these later in the chapter on pattern reading.

including . . . . incl	beginning . . . . beg
loop . . . . lp	cluster cl
pattern . . . . patt	decrease . . . . decr
preceding . . . . prec	continue . . . . cont
previous . . . . prev	cross stitch or crossed stitch . . . . cr st
remaining . . . . rem	
repeat . . . . rep	crossed treble . . . . cr tr
space . . . . sp	
stitch . . . . st	group . . . . gr or gp
yarn over hook . . . . yoh	increase . . . . incr
	across front . . . . a f
lock chain . . . . L ch	across back . . . . a b
long treble . . . . LT	front bars . . . . f b

SHAPING

DECREASING AND INCREASING DOUBLE CROCHET

The old "stairway" method of decreasing is replaced by this new method, which gives perfectly straight edges.

Make 20 chain.
Row 1 Work in dc.
Row 2 1 turning ch, 1 dc into last worked dc of prev row, draw a lp through next dc leaving it on hook, draw a lp through following dc (3 lp

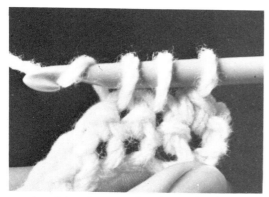

on hook), draw a lp through the 3 lp on hook (1 dc decreased), work 1 dc into every dc to last 3 dc, draw a lp through following 2 dc (3 lp on hook), draw a lp through the 3 lp on hook, work 1 dc into last dc of row.

Row 3 and following rows Cont decreasing as in row 2 until there are 5 dc in the row, then start increasing.

Increase: 1 ch, 1 dc into dc worked last in prev row, 1 dc into next dc, 1 dc into same dc (1 dc increased), 1 dc into each dc of row to last 2 dc, 2 dc into 2nd last dc, (another dc increased) 1 dc into last dc.

Continue increasing this way until there are 19 dc in the row.
Fastening off:
After working the last dc, break yarn, yoh, pull it through the rem lp on hook.

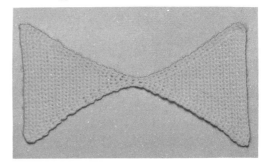

DECREASING AND INCREASING HALF TREBLE

Make 20 ch.
Row 1 1 htr into 3rd ch from hook, 1 htr into every ch to end.
Row 2 2 turning ch, 1 htr into last worked htr of prev row, *yoh, insert hook under top 2 threads of next htr, draw 1 lp through (3 lp on hook), insert hook into next htr, yoh, draw 1 lp through (4 lp on hook),

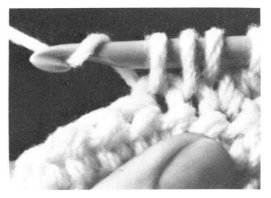

yoh, draw through the 4 lp on hook (1 htr decreased)**.

16

Work htr to rem 3 st, decr 1 htr as from * to **, 1 htr into last htr of row.

Row 3 and following rows Cont decreasing as in row 2 until there are 6 st in the row, then start increasing.

Increase: 2 turning ch, 1 htr into last worked htr in prev row, 1 htr into next htr, 1 htr into same htr, 1 htr into each htr till 2 htr remain, 2 htr into next htr, 1 htr into last htr.
Cont increasing in this way until there are 18 st in row. Fasten off.

DECREASING AND INCREASING TREBLE
Make 20 ch.
Row 1 1 tr into 4th ch from hook, 1 tr into each ch to end of row.
Row 2 3 turning ch, 1 tr into 2nd last worked tr of prev row, *yoh, draw 1 lp through next tr (3 lp on hook), yoh, draw 1 lp through 2 lp (2 lp on hook), yoh, draw 1 lp through next tr (4 lp on hook), yoh, draw 1 lp through 2 lp (3 lp on hook), yoh, draw 1 lp through the 3 lp on hook.** (1 tr decreased).

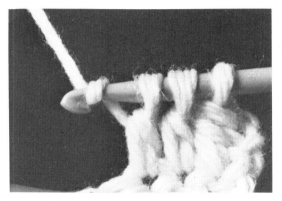

Work 1 tr into each tr till 3 st remain, rep from * to **, 1 tr into last st of row.
Row 3 and following rows Cont decreasing as in row 2 until there are

6 st in row, then start increasing as follows:

Increase: 3 turning ch, 1 tr into 2nd last worked tr of prev row, 1 tr into next tr, 1 tr into same tr, 1 tr into each tr till 2 st remain, 2 tr into next tr, 1 tr into last st. (2 treble increased in row).

Cont increasing in this way (every 2nd and 2nd last st of row) until there are 18 tr in row.
Fasten off.

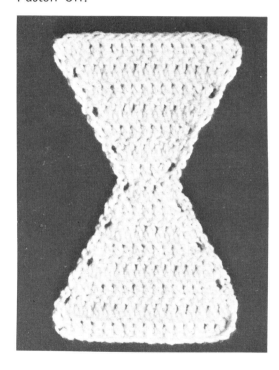

DECREASING AND INCREASING DOUBLE TREBLE

Make 30 chain.
Row 1 1 dtr into 5th ch from hook, 1 dtr into each ch to end of row.
Row 2 4 turning ch, 1 dtr into 2nd last worked dtr in prev row,
* yoh twice, insert hook into next dtr, draw 1 lp through (4 lp on hook), yoh, draw 1 lp through 2 lp (3 lp on hook), yoh, draw 1 lp through 2 lp (2 lp on hook), yoh twice, insert hook into next dtr, draw 1 lp through (5 lp on hook), yoh, draw 1 lp through 2 lp (4 lp on hook),
yoh, draw 1 lp through 2 lp (3 lp on hook),

yoh, draw 1 lp through the 3 lp on hook** (1 dtr decreased),

1 dtr into each dtr till 4 st remain, decr 1 dtr as from * to **, 1 dtr into each of the last 2 st in row.

Row 3 and following rows Cont decreasing as in row 2 until there are 5 dtr in the row, then start increasing.

Increase: 4 turning ch, 1 dtr into 2nd last worked dtr of prev row, 1 dtr into next dtr, 1 dtr into same dtr, 1 dtr into each dtr till 2 st remain in row, 2 dtr into next dtr, 1 dtr into last st (2 dtr increased in row).

Incr in dtr by working 2 dtr into the 2nd and 2 dtr into the 2nd last st in row until practice piece is increased to its original width.

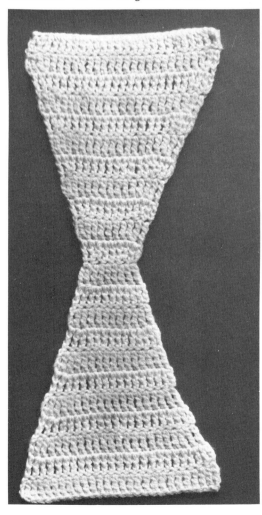

DECREASING AND INCREASING TRIPLE TREBLE

Make 30 chain.

Row 1 1 ttr into 6th ch from hook, 1 ttr into each ch to end.

Row 2 5 turning ch, 1 ttr into 2nd last worked ttr of prev row, *yoh 3 times, insert hook into next ttr, draw 1 lp through (5 lp on hook), yoh, draw 1 lp through 2 lp (4 lp on hook), yoh, draw 1 lp through 2 lp (3 lp on hook), yoh, draw 1 lp through 2 lp (2 lp on hook), yoh 3 times, insert hook into next ttr, draw 1 lp through (6 lp on hook), yoh, draw 1 lp through 2 lp (5 lp on hook), yoh, draw 1 lp through 2 lp (4 lp on hook), yoh, draw 1 lp· through 2 lp (3 lp on hook), yoh, draw 1 lp through the 3 lp on hook** (1 ttr decreased).

Work 1 ttr into each ttr till 4 st
remain, rep from * to **, 1 ttr into
each of last 2 st.

Row 3 and following rows Cont
decreasing as in row 2 until there are
6 ttr in the row, then start
increasing.

Increase: 5 turning ch, 1 ttr into
2nd last worked ttr in prev row,
1 ttr into next ttr, 1 ttr into same
ttr, 1 ttr into each of following ttr
till 2 st remain, 1 ttr into 2nd last
st, 1 ttr into same ttr, 1 ttr into
last st.
Incr in ttr by working 2 ttr into
2nd and 2 ttr into 2nd last ttr in
row until practice piece is increased
to its starting width.

READING PATTERNS

Pattern reading is not as complicated as it first looks, and with some patience and practice anyone can learn to become a skilled crocheter. But remember, for your encouragement, that even a crocheter with long pattern reading experience sometimes finds it difficult to read and interpret a pattern at first.

It is important to read slowly and carefully, observing commas, brackets ( ), asterisks (*) and other punctuation; for all these signs and their placing have a special meaning.

Read and do first what is written between the commas or the commas and full stops, then continue the work. Stitches or other instructions enclosed by brackets should be worked together, repeated together or missed together according to the instruction immediately before or after the bracket. A set of instructions to be repeated once or more may start with, or start and end with, an asterisk or asterisks.

To make pattern reading easier, and to avoid confusion when following the instructions, cover up with a postcard the text below the line you are reading.

You will notice that many pattern writers mention the turning chain at the end of the row, before the work is turned. Do not forget these chain stitches when turning — and before you start a new row, ascertain how many turning chains have to be made. The turning chain is given at the beginning of the rows in this book. There are two methods given for the working of the turning chain (see pages 9 and 13).

After crocheting the first two or three rows of your work use your measuring tape to make sure that you are working to the right tension and the measurements are correct from the beginning. It is discouraging to have to undo a half-finished piece because it is too large or too small.

As we progress further with the pattern reading it will no longer be necessary to spell out what is already obvious to you: 2 turning ch becomes simply 2 ch; ''1 st into next st, next st into same st'' is the same as ''2 st into next st''. At the end of the row you will not need to be reminded to turn the work.

If you observe the few simple rules you will find that crocheting can be great fun and a most exciting creative art. It will also help to fill many lonely hours.

Some of the commonly used terms will now be explained and illustrated. It pays to practise these and to refer back to them as needed, because we will often meet them in the exercises of this book and in other pattern instructions.

(a) **Work into the chain space** or **chain loop:** insert the hook into the space underneath or around the chain.

treble being worked into chain space

treble being worked into chain

(b) **Slip stitch to form a ring:** insert hook into the first worked chain, yoh, draw yarn right through ch and through loop on hook.

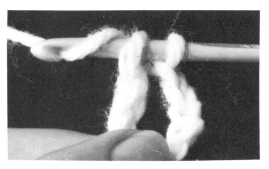

(c) **Work stitches into ring:** if the instruction reads, for example "work 10 st into ring", insert hook through the centre space of the ring for each stitch to be worked into the ring.

(d) **Work stitches into the chain stitches making up the ring:** e.g. "work 2 tr into each ch of ring". The hook is to be inserted into one loop of each ch.

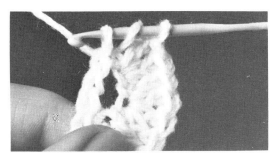

(e) **Slip stitch across stitches:** for instance, "sl st across 3 tr" means to slip stitch **into each stitch** (treble or other) — resembling casting off in knitting.

A-LINE SKIRT FROM A STRAIGHT SKIRT PATTERN

An easy way to crochet an A-line skirt is to follow a pattern for a straight skirt using five or more different sized hooks, ranging from 2.50 (old no. 12) for the waist section to, say, 4.50 (no. 7) at the hem, as illustrated.

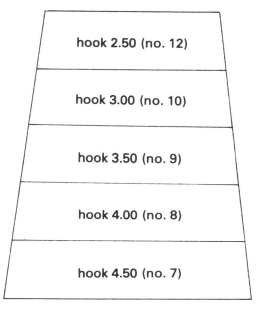

| hook 2.50 (no. 12) |
| hook 3.00 (no. 10) |
| hook 3.50 (no. 9) |
| hook 4.00 (no. 8) |
| hook 4.50 (no. 7) |

PATTERN EXERCISES

We now turn our attention to some interesting exercises in stitches and patterns. Later, when you work from patterns in magazines and crochet books, you may find that some of the names given to stitches and some of the terms employed in these publications are different from those used here, but do not be put off by this: they are invariably explained, often with illustrations. In the majority of cases there is essentially very little difference.

WORKING MOTIFS AND ROUNDS

When working motifs or rounds, as in the "cushion cover" exercise below, there is no need to turn the work when the round is completed. The new round starts with the required number of "beginning chain" in contrast to the turning chain when the article is worked in rows.

HOW TO JOIN IN A DIFFERENT COLOURED YARN

After completing the row in one colour or when the round is worked with the final slip stitches, join in the new coloured yarn with a reef knot at the back of the work, pulling it tight and leaving a length of yarn 3 to 4 cm (1½ in) long on the joining knot. Work the starting chain of the new round or the turning chain of the new row with the second colour, and do the same for each row or round of different colour. When fastening off, use a blunt wool needle and thread the yarn neatly into the back of the stitches, always into the same colour.

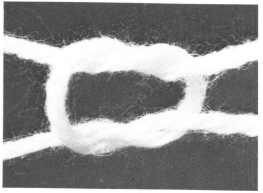

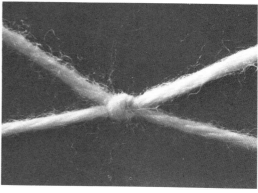

MULTI-COLOURED CUSHION COVER

Materials
Oddments of 6 ply wool, approx 200 g (7 oz). Hook 3.50 (no. 9)

Note: New colours should be joined in before the beginning chain of a round. (Change colour after every 2nd or 3rd round of the front.) There is no need to turn the work at the end of a round.

Front
Make 6 ch, join with sl st to form a ring.
Round 1 12 dc into ring, sl st to 1st dc of round.
Round 2 3 ch, 1 tr into foundation

of the 3 ch, 2 tr into each dc to end of round, sl st to upper ch at beginning of round. Join contrasting colour in now if desired, using a reef knot.

Round 3 3 ch, incr 1 tr every 3rd tr, sl st to upper ch at beginning of round.

Round 4 3 ch, incr 1 tr every 4th tr (counting the 3 ch as 1st tr), sl st to upper ch at beginning of round.

Round 5 As round 4, but incr every 5th tr.

Round 6 As round 4, but incr every 3rd tr.

Round 7 As round 4, but incr every 2nd tr.

Round 8 As round 4; but incr every 4th tr.

Round 9 As round 4, but incr every 5th tr.

Rounds 10 to 15 3 ch, 1 tr into each tr to end of round (no incr), sl st into upper beginning ch of round.

Back

Work as front, but in a single colour

To make up

Inserting hook into the edge stitches (trebles of round 15) join the two parts with a round of dc. Insert the cushion with the filling before completing the round.

Decorative picot edge

*4 dc, 1 picot (3 ch, draw yarn through 2nd ch, draw yarn through 3rd ch, draw yarn through 3 lp on hook), rep from * to end of round. Fasten off.

SHELL STITCH IN DOUBLE CROCHET AND HALF TREBLE 1

The following set of two small exercises show how minor differences in the method of working the stitches result in textures of different appearance.

Make 35 ch

Row 1 (1 dc, 1 htr) into 3rd ch from hook, *miss 1 ch, (1 dc, 1 htr) into next ch, rep from * to last 2 ch, miss 1 ch, 1 dc into last ch.

Row 2 1 ch, (1 dc, 1 htr) into 1st dc,* (1 dc, 1 htr) into space between shells, rep from * to end of row, 1 dc into turning ch.

Repeat row 2 for pattern.

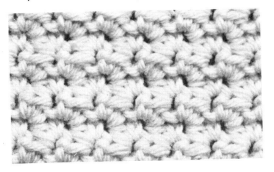

SHELL STITCH IN DOUBLE CROCHET AND HALF TREBLE 2

Make 30 ch (multiple of 3).

Row 1 (1 htr, 1 dc) into 3rd ch from hook, *1 ch, miss 2 ch, (1 htr, 1 dc) into next ch, rep from * to end of row.

Row 2 2 ch, *(1 htr, 1 dc) into next ch sp, 1 ch, rep from * to end of row, (1 htr, 1 dc) into turning ch.

Repeat row 2 for pattern.

The illustration shows how this simple stitch can be made very attractive by the use of different colours.

Colour illustration opp.   p. 38.

AN EASY LACE STITCH

Worked on a loose foundation chain.
Make 41 ch (multiple of 4 plus 1).

Row 1 1 tr into 5th ch from hook, * miss 3 ch, (1 tr, 2 ch, 1 tr) into next ch, rep from * to last 4 ch, miss 3 ch, (1 tr, 1 ch, 1 tr) into last ch.

Row 2 3 ch, 2 tr into 1st ch sp, 4 tr into each 2 ch sp to the last, 3 tr into last sp.

Row 3 3 ch, * (1 tr, 2 ch, 1 tr) in sp between tr groups, rep from * to end of row, 1 tr into upper turning ch.

Row 4 3 ch, 4 tr into each 2 ch sp to end of the row, 1 tr into upper turning ch.

Row 5 4 ch, 1 tr in sp between 1st and 2nd tr, * (1 tr, 2 ch, 1 tr) in sp between next two 4 tr groups, rep from * to last tr group, (1 tr, 1 ch, 1 tr) into turning ch.

Rep rows 2 to 5 for pattern.

This delightful lacy pattern is suitable for baby-wear, blouses, scarves and many other useful and decorative articles.

Colour illustration opp.   p. 38.

STOLE IN ATTRACTIVE LACE STITCH

Materials

750 g (26 oz) 5 or 6 ply crepe wool
Hook 3.50 (no. 9).

Measurements

Length approx. 180 cm (70 in)

26

Tension: 5 cm (2 in) over 4 3-tr groups; 5 cm (2 in) for 5 rows.

Make 101 ch.

Row 1 1 tr into 4th ch, 1 tr into next ch, *miss 1 ch, 1 ch, 1 tr into each of next 3 ch, rep from * to end.

Row 2 4 ch, 3 tr into next ch sp, *1 ch, 3 tr into next ch sp, rep from * to and including last ch sp, 1 ch, 1 tr into upper turning ch.

Row 3 3 ch, 2 tr into 1st ch sp, *1 ch, 3 tr into next ch sp, rep from * to last 4 ch sp, 2 tr into 4 ch sp, last tr into 3rd turning ch.

Row 4 4 ch, 3 tr into next ch sp, * 1 ch, 3 tr into next ch sp, rep from * to and including last ch sp, 1 ch, 1 tr into upper turning ch.

Rep rows 3 and 4 until stole is the required length.

Fringes

Cut fringes and knot into each ch sp at each end of stole as follows. Cut a piece of cardboard 14 cm long, wind the yarn around it 4 times, then cut it at the lower end. Double the length of yarn. Insert hook into 1st ch sp on short end of stole. Pull through the doubled yarn forming a loop with the hook. Draw ends of yarn through this loop and tighten the knot. Repeat, leaving two chain spaces between each fringe knot. Trim edges of fringe evenly.

AFGHAN MOTIF

(Work each round in a different colour.)

Make 5 ch and join with sl st to form a ring.

Round 1 3 ch (to stand for 1st tr), 2 tr into ring, * 2 ch, 3 tr into ring, rep from * twice, 2 ch, sl st to 3rd ch at beg of round (do not turn).

Round 2 Sl st into each of next 2 tr and into 1st sp, 3 ch, (2 tr, 2 ch, 3 tr) into same sp, *2 ch, (3 tr, 2 ch, 3 tr) into next sp, rep from * twice, 2 ch, sl st to 3rd ch at beg of round (do not turn).

Round 3 Sl st into each of next 2 tr and into 1st sp, 3 ch, (2 tr, 2 ch, 3 tr) into same sp, * 2 ch, 3 tr into next sp, 2 ch, (3 tr, 2 ch, 3 tr) into next corner sp, rep from * twice, 2 ch, 3 tr into next sp, 2 ch, sl st to 3rd ch at beg of round (do not turn).

Round 4 Sl st into each of next 2 tr and into 1st sp, 3 ch, (2 tr, 2 ch, 3 tr) into same sp, * 2 ch, 3 tr into next sp, 2 ch, 3 tr into following sp, 2 ch, (3 tr, 2 ch, 3 tr) into corner sp, rep from * twice, 2 ch, 3 tr into next sp, 2 ch, 3 tr into following sp, 2 ch, sl st to 3rd ch at beg of round.

Work a row of dc around the motif for neat edging.

Fasten off.

Colour illustration opp. p. 39.

JOINING THE MOTIFS

Afghan motifs are best joined either with slip stitches, stitch to stitch, or with a flat seam using a blunt needle and inserting it through the upper two threads of each edging stitch.

AFGHAN RUG

A beautiful rug for the home or for the car.

Materials

A total of 600 g (21 oz) *mohair* in your 3 or 4 favourite colours for a 7 by 7 square.
Hook 5.00 (no. 6).

Size of motif

Approximately 14 cm (5½ in) square, depending on tension.
Make 49 Afghan motifs and join them in rows of 7 with slip stitches, making a large square. Work 3 rounds of tr for a neat edging round the Afghan using a suitable contrasting colour, or finish with a fringe.

Colour illustration opp. p. 39.

DOUBLE TREBLE ("LONG TREBLE") LACE STITCH

Make a loose ch of 35 (odd no. of

chain, at least 13).
Row 1 1 dtr into 7th ch from hook, * 1 ch, miss 1 ch, 1 dtr into next ch, rep from * to end.
Row 2 4 ch, 1 dtr in 1st ch sp, * 2 dtr in next sp, rep from * to end.
Row 3 5 ch, 1 dtr in sp between 2nd and 3rd dtr, (counting turning ch as 1st dtr), * 1 ch, miss 2 dtr, 1 dtr in sp before next dtr, rep from * to end, working last dtr into upper turning ch.
Repeat rows 2 and 3 for pattern.

SHELL AND V PATTERN

Make 41 ch (multiple of 8 plus 1).
Row 1 1 tr into 5th ch from hook, (1 tr, 2 ch, 2 tr) into same ch, * miss 3 ch, (1 tr, 2 ch, 1 tr) into next ch, miss 3 ch, (2 tr, 2 ch, 2 tr) into next ch, rep from * to last 4 ch, miss 3 ch, 1 tr into last ch.
Row 2 3 ch, miss 3 tr, (1 tr, 2 ch, 1 tr) into 2 ch sp of 1st shell, * miss 3 tr, (2 tr, 2 ch, 2 tr) into

next 2 ch sp, miss 3 tr, (1 tr, 2 ch, 1 tr) into next 2 ch sp, rep from * to end of row, 1 tr into upper turning ch.
Row 3 3 ch, miss 2 tr, (2 tr, 2 ch, 2 tr) into next 2 ch sp, * miss 3 tr, (1 tr, 2 ch, 1 tr) into next 2 ch sp, miss 3 tr, (2 tr, 2 ch, 2 tr) into next 2 ch sp, rep from * to end, 1 tr into upper turning ch.
Rep rows 2 and 3 for pattern.

CLUNY GROUPS
("Popcorn stitch")
Worked over an even no. of ch.

Make 36 ch.
Row 1 1 dc into 2nd ch from hook, 1 dc into each ch to end of row (35 dc).
Row 2 1 ch, 1 dc into last worked dc in prev row, 1 dc into each dc to end (35 dc).
Row 3 3 ch, miss first dc, * 4 tr in next dc, take hook out and insert it under the 2 top threads of 1st tr, pick up lp of 4th tr, draw it through the top thread of 1st tr (cluny group or popcorn stitch completed), 1 ch, miss 1 dc *, cont working groups

repeating from * to * to last dc,
1 tr into last dc.

Row 4 1 ch, 1 dc into last worked
tr in prev row, * 1 dc into top of
popcorn, 1 dc into ch sp between
popcorns, rep from * to end,
working last dc into sp of turning ch
(35 dc).

Row 5 1 ch, 1 dc into last worked
dc in prev row, 1 dc into each dc
to end (35 dc).

Row 6 As row 5.

Row 7 As row 3.

Row 8 As row 4.

Rows 9 and 10 As row 5.

Row 11 As row 3.

Cluny group rows can be worked as
decorative patterns between rows of,
say, trebles for any article or
garment, as well as top rows of
pockets of a cardigan, and the rows
near the hem on skirts.

SCALLOP PATTERN
Worked over a ch of multiple of
13 plus 1.

Make 66 ch.

Row 1 1 tr into 4th ch from hook,
1 tr into each of next 4 ch, 3 tr
into next ch, 1 tr into each of next
5 ch, * miss 2 ch, 1 tr into each of
next 5 ch, 3 tr into next ch, 1 tr
into each of next 5 ch, rep from
* to end of row.

Row 2 3 ch, miss 1 tr, 1 tr into
each of next 5 tr, 3 tr into next tr,
1 tr into each of next 5 tr, * miss
2 tr, 1 tr into each of next 5 tr,
3 tr into next tr, 1 tr into each of
next 5 tr, rep from * ending miss
last tr, 1 tr into turning ch.

Note: Make sure that you have 5
treble on both the left and right
sides of the work.

Row 3 3 ch, miss 1 tr, 1 tr into
each of next 5 tr, 3 tr into next tr,
1 tr into each of next 5 tr, * miss
2 tr, 1 tr into each of next 5 tr,
3 tr into next tr, 1 tr into each of
next 5 tr, rep from * ending miss
last tr, 1 tr into turning ch.

Rep row 3 for a sample of required
height.

This pattern makes an ideal skirt
and sleeveless top for Mum and a
matching pram cover for baby.

SHELL MOTIF

Make 8 ch, sl st to 1st ch to form a ring.

Round 1 3 ch, 23 tr into ring, sl st to upper ch at beginning of round.

Round 2 6 ch, 1 tr into same place as sl st, * miss 2 tr, (1 tr, 3 ch, 1 tr) into next tr, rep from * to last 2 tr, miss 2 tr, sl st into 3rd ch at beginning of round, sl st into 3 ch space.

Round 3 3 ch, (2 tr, 3 ch, 3 tr) into 1st ch sp, * miss 2 tr, (3 tr, 3 ch, 3 tr) into next ch sp, rep from * to end of round, sl st to upper ch at beg of round, sl st into each of next 2 tr, sl st into next 3 ch sp.

Round 4 3 ch, (3 tr, 3 ch, 4 tr) into ch sp, * miss 6 tr, (4 tr, 3 ch, 4 tr) into next 3 ch sp, rep from * to end of round, sl st to 3rd upper ch at beg of round, sl st into each of next 3 tr and into ch sp.

Round 5 3 ch, (4 tr, 4 ch, 5 tr) into ch sp, * miss 8 tr, (5 tr, 4 ch, 5 tr) into next ch sp, rep from * to end of round, sl st into 3rd ch at beg.

Round 6 3 ch, 1 tr into each of next 4 tr, *(1 tr, 3 ch, 1 tr) into ch sp, 1 tr into each of next 5 tr, rep from * to last ch sp, (1 tr, 3 ch, 1 tr) into last ch sp of round, 1 tr into each of next 5 tr, sl st to 3rd ch at beg.

Round 7 4 ch, 1 dtr into each of next 2 tr, 1 tr into each of next 3 tr, (1 htr, 2ch, 1 htr) into ch sp, * 1 tr into each of next 3 tr, 1 dtr into each of next 6 tr, 1 tr into each of next 3 tr, (1 htr, 2 ch, 1 htr) into ch sp, rep from * to last

5 tr, 1 tr into each of next 3 tr, 1 dtr into each of next 3 tr, sl st to 4th ch at beg.
Fasten off.

You can make a potholder by working a row of dc around this motif and a chain loop in one corner for hanger.
Colour illustration opp.   p. 38.

MULTI-COLOURED POTHOLDER
Materials
Oddments of 8 ply wool.
Hook 4.00 (no. 8).

Note: Join in contrasting colour after slip stitching into 1st sp before working the beg ch of the new round.

Make 6 ch and join with sl st to form a ring.

Round 1 4 ch, 1 tr into ring, * (1 ch, 1 tr) into ring, rep from * 7 times, 1 ch, sl st to 3rd beg ch and into next sp. (There should be 10 trebles in this round, incl beg chain.)

Round 2 5 ch, 1 tr into 1st 1 ch sp, * (1 tr, 2 ch, 1 tr) into next 1 ch sp, rep from * to end, sl st to 3rd beg ch and into next sp.

Round 3 4 ch, (1 dtr, 2 ch, 2 dtr) into 1st sp, * (2 dtr, 2 ch, 2 dtr) into next 2 ch sp, rep from * to end of round, sl st to 4th ch, then into next dtr and into next 2 ch sp.

Round 4 5 ch, 4 ttr into 1st sp, * miss 2 dtr, (1 tr, 1 ch, 1 tr) into small sp between shells, miss 2 dtr, 5 ttr into 2 ch sp in shell, rep from * ending (1 tr, 1 ch, 1 tr) into sp between shells, sl st to 5th ch.

Round 5 3 ch, 1 tr into each of next 4 ttr, 3 dtr into 1 ch sp in "V", * 1 tr into each of next 5 ttr, 3 dtr into next 1 ch sp, rep ·from * to end, sl st to 3rd ch.

Round 6 1 ch, 1 dc into every st of round, 20 ch for hanger, 1 dc into last worked dc, sl st to next dc, pull yarn through last lp.

Thread in the loose ends of yarn into the back of work.

Note: For a doiley or coaster, work rounds 1 to 4 of this design in a 5 ply yarn. The outer shells of the coaster may be curved upwards as in the illustration.

Colour illustration opp.   p. 38.

CLUSTER MOTIF

Make a 10 ch, sl st to form a ring.

Round 1 Work 20 dc into ring, join with sl st to 1st dc at beg of round.

Round 2 1 dc into same st as sl st, * 7 ch, miss 4 dc, 1 dc into next dc, rep from * all round, ending with 7 ch, sl st into 1st dc of round.

Round 3 Sl st into 1st 7 ch lp, 3 ch, (4 tr, 5 ch, 5 tr) into same ch lp, * 1 ch, (5 tr, 5 ch, 5 tr) into next 7 ch lp, rep from * twice, 1 ch, sl st into 3rd ch.

Round 4 1 dc into last worked 1 ch sp, * 4 ch, miss 5 tr, work dtr cluster into 5 ch sp as follows: Work 1 dtr leaving top lp on hook, work 2 more dtr the same way, leaving 4 lps on hook, yoh, draw through the 4 lps on hook (cluster made), 7 ch, 1 dtr cl, 7 ch, another cl into same sp, 4 ch, miss 5 tr, 1 dc into next 1 ch sp, rep from * to end of round.

Round 5 * 4 dc into next 4 ch sp, 1 dc into cl, 7 dc into 7 ch sp, 1 dc into cl, 7 dc into next 7 ch sp, 1 dc into cl, 4 dc into next 4 ch sp, rep from * to end of round, sl st to 1st dc.

Colour illustration opp.   p. 38.

TWO-TONE CROCHET

Worked over a chain of multiple of 3 plus 2; a smart pattern for many purposes, particularly small children's wear.

Make 29 ch in colour chosen for contrast.

Row 1 1 dc into 5th ch from hook for 1st sp, * 2 ch, miss 2 ch, 1 dc into next ch, rep from * to end of ch, work last lp of the last dc in main colour, turn.

Row 2 3 ch (in main colour), * 2 tr into next 2 ch sp, rep from * to last sp, 3 tr into this sp (the 2 tr groups will be called shells).
Pull up the last lp on hook, pass the ball of yarn through this last lp to fasten off, pull it tightly, but do not break yarn. You should have 9 shells altogether. Do not turn for the next row.
Row 3 Pick up contrasting colour at beg of last row, insert hook into upper beg ch, yoh, draw through ch, 4 ch, * 1 dc between next 2 shells, 2 ch, rep from * to last shell, 1 dc into last tr of row working the last lp of the dc with main colour, turn. Rep rows 2 and 3 for pattern.

Colour illustration opp. p. 38.

WATER-LILY
Make 7 ch and join with sl st to form a ring.
Round 1 Work 16 dc into ring, sl st to dc at beg of round.
Round 2 * 5 ch, miss 1 dc, 1 dc into next dc, rep from * ending 5 ch, sl st to 1st dc of round (you now have eight 5 ch loops).
Round 3 (1 dc, 5 tr, 1 dc) into each ch lp, sl st to 1st dc at beg.

Round 4 Curve petal downwards towards you to reach the wrong side of the work, 1 dc around 1st dc of 2nd round from back, * 6 ch, 1 dc around next dc of 2nd round between petals * work in same direction as for round 3, rep from * to * ending 6 ch, sl st to dc at beg (eight 6 ch loops).
Round 5 Do not turn, with right side of work facing, (1 dc, 6 tr 1 dc) into each 6 ch lp, sl st to dc at beg.
Fasten off.

Water-lilies are used mainly as decorations on cushions and pram covers.
Colour illustration opp. p. 38.

FLOWER MOTIF
Make 12 ch and join with sl st to form a ring.
Round 1 3 ch (to be counted as 1st tr of round), work 23 tr into ring, sl st to 3rd ch.
Round 2 * 6 ch, miss 2 tr, 1 dc into next tr, rep from * to end, joining last lp with sl st to 1st ch of round (8 loops).
Round 3 Into each 6 ch lp work

(1 dc, 1 ch, 1 tr, 1 ch, 1 dtr,
1 picot (work picot as 3 ch, sl st to
1st ch), 1 dtr, 1 ch, 1 tr, 1 ch,
1 dc) sl st to 1st dc at beg.
Fasten off.

This motif is very useful for scarves,
bedspreads, ladies' garments, such as
tops.

CLUSTER PATTERN HAIRBAND
(Puff stitch)

Materials
Oddments of 8 ply wool in main
colour (A) and contrasting colour (B).
Hook 3.50 (no. 9).

Using A, make an uneven number of
chain to fit head size.
Row 1 1 dc into 2nd ch from hook,
1 dc into each ch to end.
Row 2 3 ch, miss last dc of prev
row, 1 cluster (cl, also called puff
stitch) into next dc worked as
follows:
yoh, insert hook into dc,
yoh, draw through dc (3 lp on
hook),
yoh, insert hook into same dc,
yoh, draw through (5 lp),
yoh, insert hook into same dc,
yoh, draw through (7 lp),
yoh, draw through 6 lp (2 lp left
on hook),
yoh, draw through 2 lp (cluster
completed);
* 1 ch, miss 1 dc, 1 cl into next
dc, rep from * to last 2 dc, 1 ch,
miss 1 dc, 1 tr into last dc.

Row 3 Join in B, 3 ch, 1 cl into
1st ch sp, * 1 ch, 1 cl into next ch

sp, rep from * to last cl, 1 ch, miss
1 cl, 1 tr into 3rd ch.
Row 4 Join in A, 3 ch, 1 cl into
1st ch sp, * 1 ch, 1 cl into next
1 ch sp, rep from * to last cl, 1 ch,
miss 1 cl, 1 tr into 3rd ch.
Row 5 1 ch, * 1 dc into ch sp,
1 dc into top of cl, rep from * to
end, 1 dc into 3rd ch.

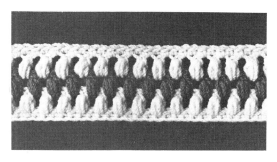

To finish off
Using a wool needle, thread the loose
ends through on the wrong side, then
stitch the short sides of the band
together with an overlap seam.

TREBLE-STITCH SCARF
Materials
350 g (13 oz) 6 ply crepe wool.
Hook 3.50 (no. 9).

Tension: 2.5 cm (1 in) to 2 rows; 2.5 cm (1 in) to one 3 tr group and 1 sp.

Make 622 ch.

Row 1 1 tr into 4th ch from hook, 1 tr into next ch, * 2 ch, miss 2 ch, 1 tr into each of next 3 ch*, rep from * to * until there are 62 3-tr groups, miss 4 ch, 1 tr into each of next 3 ch (forming a corner), then rep from * to * again (as in 1st half of row) to end, (62 3-tr gr in 2nd half of row).

Row 2 3 ch, 3 tr into next 2 ch sp, * 2 ch, 3 tr into next 2 ch sp *, rep from * to * until there is one less 3-tr gr than in first half of prev row (61 groups for row 2), miss 6 tr, 3 tr into next 2 ch sp, rep from * to * until there is the same no of gr in the 2nd half of the row as in the 1st half, 1 tr into 3rd ch.

Row 3 3 ch, 3 tr into next 2 ch sp, * 2 ch, 3 tr into next 2 ch sp, * rep from * to * until there is one less group than in 1st half of prev row (60 for row 3), miss 6 tr, 3 tr into next 2 ch sp, rep from * to * to end of row (same no. of gr as in 1st half), 1 tr into 3rd ch.

Rows 4 to 7 As row 3, each row will have one gr less at each end as you decrease the centre two 3-tr gr.

Row 8 4 ch, 2 dtr into next 2 ch sp, * 2 ch, 2 dtr into next 2 ch sp *, rep from * to * to centre, miss two groups, 2 dtr into next 2 ch sp, rep from * to * to end of row, 1 dtr into turning ch.

Row 9 Work as row 8, the 2 groups missed at centre will be 4 dtr.

Row 10 3 ch, 3 tr into next 2 ch sp, * 2 ch, 3 tr into next 2 ch sp * rep from * to * to centre of row, miss 4 dtr, 3 tr into next 2 ch sp, rep from * to * to end of row, 1 tr into turning ch.

Rows 11 to 13 As row 3.

Rows 14 and 15 2-dtr gr rows, as for rows 8 and 9. Cont to dec 2 centre grs as before.

Rows 16 to 27 3-tr gr rows.

Rows 28 and 29 2-dtr gr rows.

Row 30 onwards Work the rem rows in 3-tr groups, dec as before, until all sts are dec, ending at centre of long side.

Work a row of dc right round the scarf.

Fringes

Make fringes and knot one into each alternate 2 ch sp through the two shorter sides of the triangle and into each corner. Take half the yarns of each fringe and complete work by knotting these to adjacent half into a new fringe as illustrated.

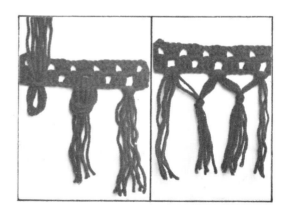

CROSSED TREBLE STITCH
Multiple of 4 plus 5.

Make 45 ch.

Row 1 yoh twice, insert hook into 6th ch from hook, * yoh, draw through ch (4 lp on hook),

yoh, draw through 2 lp, yoh once,

miss 2 ch, insert hook into next ch,

yoh, draw through ch (5 lp on hook),

(yoh, draw through 2 lp) 4 times,

2 ch, yoh, insert hook into 2 front threads in centre of cross,

yoh, draw through these 2 threads, (yoh, draw through 2 lp) twice

(crossed treble completed), yoh twice, insert hook into next ch *, rep from * to * to last ch, 1 dtr into last ch.

Row 2 5 ch, *yoh twice, insert hook into next tr, yoh, draw through, yoh, draw through 2 lp, miss 2 ch, yoh, insert hook into 2nd tr of cr tr, yoh, draw through, (yoh, draw through 2 lp) 4 times, 2 ch, yoh, insert hook into 2 threads in centre of cr tr, yoh, draw through, (yoh, draw through 2 lp) twice, rep from * to end, 1 dtr into turning ch.
Rep row 2 to required height.

A stitch for crocheting beachtops, bedspreads, cushions, hairbands and many other articles; on its own or in combination with other stitch rows.

HAIRBAND IN CROSSED TREBLE STITCH
Materials
One 25 g (1 oz) ball of 5 ply yarn. Hook 3.00 (no. 10).

Make ch to fit head size, in multiple of 4 plus 5 stitches.
Work 2 rows of cr tr.
Sew the band together at the short ends, work 2 rows of dc round both edges of the band. Thread the loose ends of yarn neatly into the wrong side of the work. This hairband looks particularly attractive if a contrasting coloured ribbon is threaded through the holes between the crossed trebles.

SPIDER PATTERN
Worked over a multiple of 14 plus 5 ch.

Make a loose ch of 61.
Row 1 1 tr into 4th ch from hook, 1 tr into every ch to end.

Row 2 3 ch, 1 tr into each of next 2 tr, * 5 ch (miss 1 tr, 1 dtr into next tr), 5 times, 5 ch, miss 1 tr, 1 tr into each of next 3 tr, rep from * to end, last tr into turning ch.

Row 3 3 ch, 1 tr into each of next 2 tr, * 4 ch, miss 5 ch, 1 dc into each of next 5 dtr, 4 ch, miss 5 ch, 1 tr into each of next 3 tr, rep from * to end, last tr into turning ch.

Row 4 3 ch, 1 tr into each of next 2 tr, * 4 ch, miss 4 ch, 1 dc into each of next 5 dc, 4 ch, miss 4 ch, 1 tr into next 3 tr, rep from * to end, last tr into turning ch.

Rows 5 and 6 As row 4.

Row 7 3 ch, 1 tr into each of next 2 tr, * 5 ch, miss 4 ch, 1 dc into each of next 5 dc, 5 ch, miss 4 ch, 1 tr into each of next 3 tr, rep from * to end, last tr into turning ch.

Row 8 3 ch, 1 tr into each of next 2 tr, * 2 ch, miss 5 ch, 1 dtr into next dc, (1 ch, 1 dtr into next dc) 4 times, 2 ch, 1 tr into each of next 3 tr, rep from * to end, last tr into turning ch.

Row 9 3 ch, 1 tr into every st of row.

This is a design with patterns of squares in which there is no need to sew individual motifs together. It can be used with beautiful effect for bedspreads, cot covers, cushions, hairbands, belts and many other garments or decorative articles.

TEAPOT LACE

Worked on a loose foundation chain of multiple of 12 plus 9.

Make 45 ch.

Row 1 1 tr into 4th ch from hook, 1 tr into each of next 5 ch, * 9 ch, miss 5 ch, 1 tr into each next 7 ch, rep from * to end.

Row 2 3 ch, 1 tr into each of next 6 tr, * 5 ch, miss 9 ch, 1 tr into each of next 7 tr, rep from * working last tr into turning ch at end (there should be 7 tr at end of row).

Row 3 3 ch, 1 tr into each of next 6 tr, * 4 ch, 1 dc around 2 lengths of ch of 2 prev rows, 4 ch, 1 tr into each of next 7 tr, rep from * to end, last tr into turning ch.

Row 4 3 ch, 1 tr into each next 6 tr, * 5 ch, 1 tr into each next 7 tr, rep from * to end, last tr into turning ch.

Row 5 12 ch, miss 5 tr, 1 tr into next tr, 1 tr into each of next 5 ch, 1 tr into next tr, * 9 ch, miss 5 tr, 1 tr into next tr, 1 tr into each of next 5 ch, 1 tr into next tr, rep from * to last 6 tr, 9 ch, miss 6 tr, 1 tr into turning ch.

Row 6 8 ch, miss 9 ch, 1 tr into each of next 7 tr, * 5 ch, 1 tr into each of next 7 tr, rep from * ending with 5 ch, miss 8 ch, 1 tr into next ch.

Row 7 7 ch, 1 dc around 2 lengths of ch of 2 prev rows, 4 ch, 1 tr into each next 7 tr, * 4 ch, 1 dc around 2 lengths of ch of 2 prev rows, 4 ch, 1 tr into each of next 7 tr, rep from * to last 8 ch loop, 4 ch, 1 dc around 2 lengths of ch of 2 prev rows, 4 ch, 1 tr into 3rd turning ch.

Row 8 8 ch, miss (4 ch, 1 dc, 4 ch), * 1 tr into each of next 7 tr, 5 ch, rep from * to last (4 ch, 1 dc, 4 ch), miss (4 ch, 1 dc, 4 ch), 1 tr into next ch.

Row 9 3 ch, 1 tr into each of next 5 ch, 1 tr into next tr, * 9 ch, miss 5 tr, 1 tr into next tr, 1 tr into each of next 5 ch, 1 tr into next tr, rep from * to end, last tr into turning ch.

Repeat rows 2 to 9 for pattern.

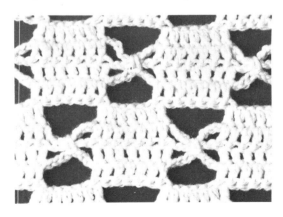

FAN STITCH LACE
Make 43 ch (multiple of 10 plus 13).
Row 1 1 tr into 4th ch from hook, * 1 ch, miss 3 ch, (1 tr, 3 ch, 1 tr)

into next ch, 1 ch, miss 3 ch, 1 tr into each of next 3 ch, rep from * to last 9 ch, 1 ch, miss 3 ch, (1 tr, 3 ch, 1 tr) into next ch, 1 ch, miss 3 ch, 1 tr into each of last 2 ch.

Row 2 4 ch, * miss (1 tr, 1 ch, 1 tr), work 7 tr into next 3 ch sp, 1 ch, miss (1 tr, 1 ch, 1 tr), 1 tr into next tr, 1 ch, rep from * to end, tr into turning ch.

Row 3 4 ch, 1 tr into last worked tr in prev row, * 1 ch, miss (1 ch, 2 tr), 1 tr into each of next 3 tr, 1 ch, miss (2 tr, 1 ch), (1 tr, 3 ch, 1 tr) into next tr, rep from * ending with (1 tr, 1 ch, 1 tr) into turning ch.

Row 4 3 ch, 3 tr into 1st ch sp, * 1 ch, miss (1 tr, 1 ch, 1 tr), 1 tr into next tr, 1 ch, miss (1 tr, 1 ch, 1 tr), 1 ch, 7 tr into next 3 ch sp, rep from * ending 4 tr into last ch. sp .

Row 5 3 ch, 1 tr into next tr, * 1 ch, miss (2 tr, 1 ch), (1 tr, 3 ch, 1 tr) into next tr, 1 ch, miss (1 ch, 2 tr), 1 tr into each of next 3 tr, rep from * ending 1 tr into last tr, 1 tr into turning ch.

Repeat rows 2 to 5 for pattern.

38

a. Shell stitch in double crochet and half treble (2) (p. 25).
b. An easy lace stitch (p. 26). c. A pot holder using the shell motif (p. 30).
d. A multi-coloured pot holder (p. 31). e. Cluster motif (p. 31).
f. Two-tone crochet (p. 31). g. Water-lily (p. 32).

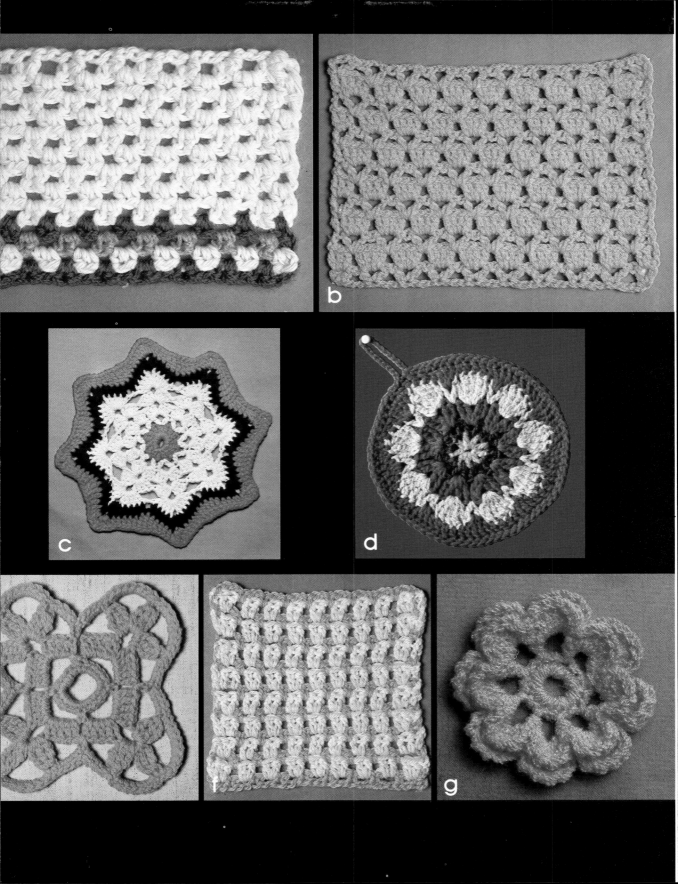

b

c

d

f

g

SHELL PATTERN

An exercise for increasing within the shell.

Make 37 ch.

Row 1 1 tr into 4th ch from hook, 1 tr into next ch, 2 ch, 1 tr into each of next 2 ch, * miss 1 ch, 1 tr into next ch, miss 1 ch, 1 tr into each of next 2 ch, 2 ch, 1 tr into each of next 2 ch, rep from * to last 2 ch, miss 1 ch, 1 tr into last ch.

Row 2 3 ch, miss 2 tr, (2 tr, 2 ch, 2 tr) into next 2 ch sp, * miss 2 tr, 1 tr into next tr, miss 2 tr, (2 tr, 2 ch, 2 tr) into next 2 ch sp, rep from * ending miss 2 tr, 1 tr into turning ch.

Rows 3 and 4 As row 2.

Row 5 (incr row) 3 ch, miss 2 tr, (3 tr, 3 ch, 3 tr) into next 2 ch sp, * miss 2 tr, 1 tr into next tr, miss 2 tr, (3 tr, 3 ch, 3 tr) into next 2 ch sp, rep from * ending miss 2 tr, 1 tr into turning ch.

Row 6 3 ch, miss 3 tr, (3 tr, 3 ch, 3 tr) into next 3 ch sp, * miss 3 tr, 1 tr into next tr, miss 3 tr, (3 tr, 3 ch, 3 tr) into next 3 ch sp, rep from * ending miss 3 tr, 1 tr into turning ch.

Rows 7 to 9 As row 6.

Row 10 (incr row) 3 ch, miss 3 tr, (4 tr, 3 ch, 4 tr) into next 3 ch sp, * miss 3 tr, 1 tr into next tr, miss 3 tr, (4 tr, 3 ch, 4 tr) into next 3 ch sp, rep from * ending miss 3 tr, 1 tr into turning ch.

Row 11 3 ch, miss 4 tr, (4 tr, 3 ch, 4 tr) into next 3 ch sp, * miss 4 tr, 1 tr into next tr, miss 4 tr, (4 tr, 3 ch, 4 tr) into next 3 ch sp, rep from * ending miss 4 tr, 1 tr into turning ch.

Row 12 (incr row) 3 ch, miss 4 tr, (5 tr, 4 ch, 5 tr) into next 3 ch sp, * miss 4 tr, 1 tr into next tr, miss 4 tr, (5 tr, 4 ch, 5 tr) into next 3 ch sp, rep from * ending miss 4 tr, 1 tr into turning ch.

Row 13 3 ch, miss 5 tr, (5 tr, 4 ch, 5 tr) into next 4 ch sp, * miss 5 tr, 1 tr into next tr, miss 5 tr, (5 tr, 4 ch, 5 tr) into next 4 ch sp, rep from * ending miss 5 tr, 1 tr into turning ch.

This method of increasing is very useful for making a flared skirt, starting at the waist and working downwards.

THREE EDGINGS FOR WOVEN FABRIC

Edgings for woven articles (tablecloth, garments, handkerchief, blanket, and so on) are best crocheted on to a foundation stitch and not into the edge of the material itself, for even a fine crochet hook could tear the fabric. Such foundation stitch could be a blanket stitch or similar stitches which produce a regular loop.

Using a sewing needle and the yarn to be used for the crochet edge, make the blanket (or other) stitch edge the same number of loops as the number of stitches needed for the crochet foundation row. This foundation row for the pattern is often a dc row, but may also be a tr row.

There are three edgings illustrated here, with instructions for practice pieces. These little samples are worked over chain.

1. Full Picot Edge
Worked over a chain of multiple of 3 plus 2 (or over a multiple of 3 foundation edging stitches).

Make 23 ch.
Row 1 1 dc into 2nd ch, 1 dc into each ch to end.
Row 2 1 ch, 1 dc, * 4 ch, yoh, insert hook into 3rd ch from hook, yoh, draw through ch, yoh, draw through 2 loops, insert hook into next ch, yoh, draw through ch (3 lp on hook), yoh, draw through the 3 lp (1 full picot made), miss 2 dc, 1 dc into next dc, rep from * to end.

2. Picot Edge
Multiple of 3 plus 1 ch or multiple of 3 foundation edging st.

Make 22 ch.
Row 1 1 dc into 2nd ch, 1 dc into

each ch to end.
Row 2 1 ch, 3 dc, * 3 ch, sl st into 1st of the 3 ch, (picot made) 3 dc, rep from * to end.
The number of dc stitches between the picots in a picot edge pattern may be varied as required.

3. Shell Edge
Multiple of 6 plus 2 ch or multiple of 6 foundation edging st.

Make 32 ch.
Row 1 1 dc into 2nd ch, 1 dc into each ch to end.
Row 2 1 ch, 1 dc into 1st dc, * miss next 2 dc, 7 tr into next dc, miss 2 dc, 1 dc into next dc, rep from * to end.

CROCHET-COVERED BUTTON

Materials
Round button of suitable size for covering.
Oddment 5 ply wool.
Hook 2.50 (no. 12).

Make 4 ch, join with sl st to form a ring.
Round 1 8 dc into ring.
Round 2 2 dc into each dc of round 1.
Round 3 1 dc into 1st dc, 2 dc into next dc, * 1 dc into next dc, 2 dc into following dc, rep from * to end.
Round 4 and onwards Rep round 3 until piece measures same as button.
Decr round * 1 dc, draw a lp through next dc, draw a lp through following dc, draw a lp through the 3 lp on hook (1 dc decreased), rep from * to end.
Cont decr to end rounds, place the button in the crochet cover after the 2nd decr round.
Cont decr until button is completely covered.
Fasten off.

It is now easy to sew the button on, using the same yarn either through the holes in the button or through the back of the cover.

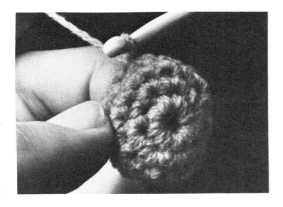

BUTTONHOLES
Make 28 ch.
Row 1 1 dc into 2nd ch from hook, 1 dc into each ch to end.

Row 2 1 ch, 1 dc into last worked dc in prev row, 1 dc into each dc to end (27 dc).
Row 3 1 ch, 4 dc, 3 ch, miss 3 dc, 1 dc into next dc, 1 dc into each of next 4 dc, 3 ch, miss 3 dc, 1 dc into next dc, 1 dc into each of next 4 dc, 3 ch, miss 3 dc, 1 dc into next dc, 1 dc into each of next 3 dc.
Row 4 1 ch, 1 dc into last worked dc in prev row, 1 dc into each of next 3 dc, 3 dc into 3 ch sp (1 buttonhole completed), 1 dc into each of next 5 dc, 3 dc into 3 ch sp, 1 dc into each of next 5 dc, 3 dc into 3 ch sp, 1 dc into each of last 4 dc.
Row 5 1 ch, 1 dc into each dc to end. (Sample A)

BUTTON LOOPS
Make 32 ch for a practice piece with different button loops.
Row 1 1 dc into 2nd ch from hook, 1 dc into each ch to end.
Row 2 1 ch, 1 dc into last worked dc in prev row, 1 dc into each dc to end.
Row 3 and 4 As row 2.
Row 5 1 ch, 1 dc into last worked dc in prev row, 1 dc into each of next 2 dc, 10 ch, miss 4 dc, 1 dc into next dc, 1 dc into each of next 2 dc, 8 ch, 1 dc into next dc, 1 dc into each dc to end.
Row 6 1 ch, 1 dc into last worked dc in prev row, 1 dc into next dc. * 3 ch, miss 2 dc, 1 dc into each of next 3 dc, rep from * to 8 ch lp, 12 dc into 8 ch lp, 1 dc into each of next 3 dc, 16 dc into 10

ch lp, 1 dc into each of last 3 dc.
(Sample C)

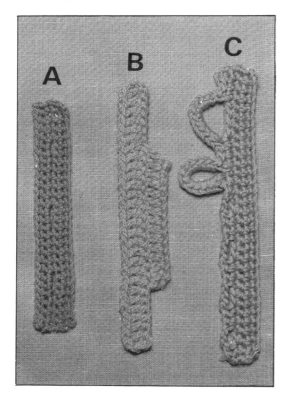

ADDING SIDE TREBLES
This useful little exercise shows you
how to add trebles evenly to both
sides of a crocheted garment.
Start the practice piece with 20 ch
and work 2 rows of tr.
Add 10 ch to the 2nd row of tr,
turn, work 1 tr into 4th ch from
hook, 1 tr into each ch and into
each following tr, last tr into upper
turning ch (you should have 7 tr
plus the turning ch on the right side
of the work).
Now add 8 tr to the left side of the
sample piece as follows:
yoh, insert hook into the same
turning ch as for last tr, yoh, draw

through ch, yoh, draw through the
lowest lp as if you were making a
ch, (yoh, draw through 2 lp) twice
* yoh, insert hook into 2 lowest
threads of extra ch worked at the
foundation of last tr, yoh, draw
through these 2 lower threads, yoh,
draw through the lower lp (1
foundation ch made), yoh, draw
through 2 lp, yoh, draw through 2 lp
again, rep from * 6 times (8 tr
added to left side of work). (Sample B)

Remember this exercise particularly
when you are crocheting a bikini.

JOINING SEAMS
There are three basic types of seams
for joining the parts of a crocheted
garment: the overlap seam, the flat
seam and the double crochet seam.

1. Overlap seam
The pieces to be joined are held
together with the right sides facing
inwards. Sew them together
uniformly, making sure that no holes
appear at the seam after joining
("oversewn seam").

Alternatively, instead of sewing with
the wool needle, the overlap seam

may be joined with slip stitches using the same crocheting hook as for the rest of the work.

2. Flat seam

The two pieces to be joined should be laid flat, seam edge to seam edge, and the corresponding pattern rows joined by sewing them together.

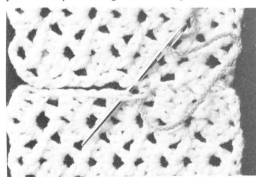

3. Double crochet seam

This is a useful and neat method of joining and is used generally with fine yarns. It is also easy to unpick if necessary.

The pieces to be joined are held together as for the overlap or over-sewn seam. It is made by working 2 dc around the outer tr of corresponding rows in the seam;

work 1 dc for rows ending in dc,
  3 dc for dtr rows and
  4 dc for ttr rows.

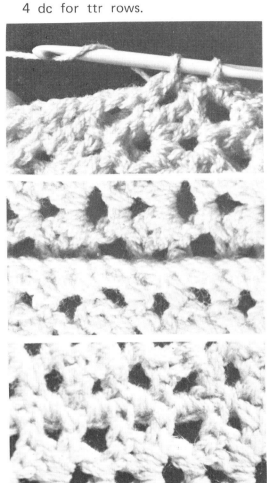

SLEEVE-TOP AND ARMHOLE SHAPING

A perfect fit in a crocheted garment requires a properly shaped sleeve top and armhole.

In double crochet and treble patterns the method of decreasing in the 2nd and 3rd stitches and the 2nd and 3rd last stitches of a row may be followed. This is described in the exercises for increasing and decreasing.

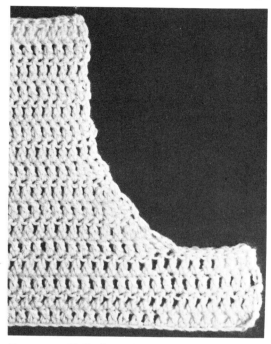

For a well-fitting shape to an armhole and sleeve of a lace-pattern crochet garment, work an extra treble at the end of each pattern row and 3 chain for turning at the beginning of rows. This will give a firm, even edge round both the sleeve top and the armhole edge.

The following two practice pieces are examples of this method.

1. A Sleeve-top Shaping exercise
Make a 55 ch.

Row 1 (1 tr, 3 ch, 1 tr) into 4th ch from hook, * 1 ch, miss 3 ch, 1 tr into each of next 3 ch, 1 ch, miss 3 ch, (1 tr, 3 ch, 1 tr) into next ch, rep from * to end, 1 tr into last ch.

Row 2 3 ch, miss 1 tr, 5 tr into next 3 ch sp, * 1 ch, 1 tr into middle of 3 tr gr, 1 ch, miss (1 tr, 1 ch, 1 tr), 5 tr into 3 ch sp, rep from * to end, 1 ch, 1 tr into turning ch.

Row 3 4 ch, miss 1 tr, 1 tr into each of next 3 tr, * miss (1 tr, 1 ch), 1 ch, (1 tr, 3 ch, 1 tr) into next tr, 1 ch, miss (1 ch, 1 tr), 1 tr into each of next 3 tr, rep from * to last tr, miss 1 tr, 1 tr into turning ch.

Row 4 5 ch, 1 tr into 2nd tr of 3 tr group, 1 ch, * 5 tr into 3 ch sp, 1 ch, 1 tr into 2nd tr of 3 tr gr, 1 ch, rep from * to end, 1 ch, last tr into turning ch.

Decrease rows

Row 5 Sl st into each of next 7 st, 3 ch, 1 tr into 4th tr of 5 tr shell, * miss (1 tr, 1 ch), 1 ch, (1 tr, 3 ch, 1 tr) into next tr, 1 ch, miss (1 ch, 1 tr), 1 tr into each of next 3 tr, rep from * to before last shell, miss (1 ch, 1 tr), 1 tr into each of next 2 tr, turn.

Row 6 4 ch, 5 tr into next 3 ch sp, miss (1 tr, 1 ch, 1 tr), * 1 ch, 1 tr into 2nd tr of 3 tr gr, 1 ch, miss (1 tr, 1 ch, 1 tr), 5 tr into 3 ch sp, rep from * to last 2 tr, miss 2 tr, 1 tr into turning ch.

Row 7 3 ch, miss 1 tr, 1 tr into each of next 3 tr, * 1 ch, miss (1 tr, 1 ch,), (1 tr, 3 ch, 1 tr) into next tr, 1 ch, miss (1 ch, 1 tr), 1 tr into each of next 3 tr, rep from * to last tr, miss 1 tr (in last shell), 1 tr into turning ch.

Row 8 3 ch, 1 tr into 2nd tr of 3 tr gr, miss (1 tr, 1 ch, 1 tr), * 1 ch, 5 tr into 3 ch sp, 1 ch,

miss (1 tr, 1 ch, 1 tr), 1 tr into
2nd tr of 3 tr gr, rep from * to last
tr, miss 1 tr, 1 tr into turning ch.

Row 9 5 ch, miss (1 tr, 1 ch, 1 tr),
* 1 tr into each of next 3 tr, 1 ch,
miss (1 tr, 1 ch), (1 tr, 3 ch, 1 tr)
into next tr, miss (1 ch, 1 tr), 1 ch,
rep from * ending 1 tr in next 3 tr,
1 ch, miss (1 tr, 1 ch, 1 tr), 1 tr
into turning ch.

Row 10 4 ch, miss (1 ch, 1 tr), 1 tr
into 2nd tr in 3 tr gr, 1 ch, miss
(1 tr, 1 ch, 1 tr), * 5 tr into 3 ch
sp, 1 ch, miss (1 tr, 1 ch, 1 tr),
1 tr into 2nd tr in 3 tr gr, 1 ch,
rep from * once, miss (1 tr, 2ch),
1 tr into turning ch.

Row 11 4 ch, miss (1 tr, 1 ch,
1 tr), 1 tr into each of next 3 tr,
miss (1 tr, 1 ch), 1 ch, (1 tr,
3 ch, 1 tr) into next tr, 1 ch, miss
(1 ch, 1 tr), 1 tr into each of next
3 tr, miss (1 tr, 1 ch, 1 tr), 1 tr
into turning ch.

Row 12 4 ch, 1 tr into 2nd tr in
3 tr gr, miss (1 tr, 1 ch, 1 tr),
1 ch, 5 tr into 3 ch sp, 1 ch, miss
(1 tr, 1 ch, 1 tr), 1 tr into 2nd tr
in 3 tr gr, miss (1 tr, 1 ch), 1 tr
into turning ch.
Fasten off.

2. Armhole Shaping Exercise
Make 34 ch.

Row 1 (2 tr, 2 ch, 2 tr) into 6th
ch, * miss 3 ch, (2 tr, 2 ch, 2 tr)
into next ch, rep from * to last
4 ch, miss 3 ch, 1 tr into last ch.

Row 2 3 ch, miss 2 tr, (2 tr, 2 ch,
2 tr) into next 2 ch sp in shell,
* miss 4 tr, (2 tr, 2 ch, 2 tr) into
next shell, rep from * to last 2 tr,
1 tr into turning ch.

Row 3 (start of decreasing) 1 ch,
1 htr into next tr, 2 dc into 2 ch
sp, 1 ch, 1 tr between 1st and 2nd
shells, 4 ch, 2 tr into 2 ch sp of
2nd shell, * (2 tr, 2 ch, 2 tr) into
next shell, rep from * to end, 1 tr
into turning ch.

Row 4 3 ch, 5 shells, miss 3 tr,
1 tr into last tr.

Row 5 4 ch, 2 tr into 1st shell,
4 shells, 1 tr into turning ch.

Row 6 3 ch, 4 shells, miss 4 tr,
1 tr into turning ch.

Row 7 3 ch, 4 shells, 1 tr into
turning ch.

Rows 8 to 10 As row 7.

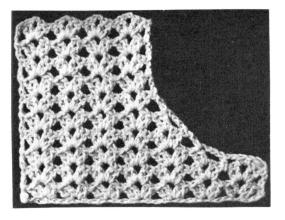

MAKING A DRESS

BELL-PATTERN DRESS

Materials
350 g (13 oz) 6 ply crepe wool or cotton in main colour.
50 g (2 oz) in contrasting colour.
Hook 3.00 (no. 10).
Tension: 8 tr for 5 cm (2 in), 2 tr rows for 2.5 cm (1 in).

Measurements
To fit 86 cm (34 in) bust, 66 cm (26 in) waist and 90 cm (35 in) hip. For other sizes please see note at the end of this pattern.

Skirt
Note: The skirt is worked from the waist down. The first bells are formed with the completion of the 4th round. Each 3-round group, starting from rounds 2, 3 and 4, forms a row of bells. The 10th, 12th, 13th and 15th bell rows are worked in contrasting colour and all other rounds and rows of the dress are worked in main colour.

Make 172 ch (multiple of 9 plus 1).
Round 1 1 tr into 4th ch from hook, 1 tr into each of next 2 ch, (1 tr, 3 ch, 1 tr) into next ch, 1 tr into each next 3 ch, * miss 2 ch, 1 tr into each of next 3 ch, (1 tr, 3 ch, 1 tr) into next ch, 1 tr into each of next 3 ch, rep from * to end, sl st to ch at beg of row to form a round, sl st into each of next 3 tr and into 3 ch sp. Do not turn.
Round 2 (3 ch, 6 tr) into 1st 3 ch sp, * 7 ch, miss 8 tr, 7 tr into next 3 ch sp, rep from * ending 7 ch, 1 dc to ch at beg of round.

Round 3 1 dc into each of next 6 tr, * 3 ch, 1 tr inserting hook into sp between the two 4 tr groups in 1st round and also working around 7 ch lp of 2nd round, 3 ch, 1 dc into each of next 7 tr, rep from * to last 7 ch lp, 3 ch, 1 tr inserting hook between the open two 4 tr gr and round 7 ch lp, 3 ch, sl st to 1st dc of round.
Round 4 3 ch, 1 tr into each of next 2 dc, (1 tr, 3 ch, 1 tr) into next dc, 1 tr into each of next 3 dc, * 5 ch, 1 tr into each of next 3 dc, (1 tr, 3 ch, 1 tr) into next dc, 1 tr into each of next 3 dc, rep from * to end, 5 ch, sl st to beg ch.
Round 5 Sl st into each of next 3 tr and into 1st 3 ch sp, (3 ch, 6 tr) into same 3 ch sp, * 7 ch, miss (4 tr, 5 ch, 4 tr), 7 tr into next 3 ch sp, rep from * ending 7 ch, 1 dc into beg ch.
Round 6 1 dc into each of next 6 tr, * 3 ch, 1 tr around lengths of ch of 2 prev rounds, 3 ch, 1 dc into each of next 7 tr, rep from * to last ch sp, 3 ch, 1 tr around ch lengths, 3 ch, sl st to 1st dc at beg of round.
Round 7 3 ch, 1 tr into each of next 2 dc, (1 tr, 3 ch, 1 tr) into next dc, 1 tr into each of next 3 dc, 5 ch, * 1 tr into each of next 3 dc, (1 tr, 3 ch, 1 tr) into next dc, 1 tr into each of next 3 dc, 5 ch, rep from * to end, sl st to beg ch.
Rounds 8 to 22 Rep rounds 5 to 7 five times, thus completing 7 bell rows.
Round 23 Sl st into each of next 3 tr and into 1st 3 ch sp, 3 ch, 8 tr into same 3 ch sp, 9 ch, * miss

(4 tr, 5 ch, 4 tr), 9 tr into next 3 ch sp, 9 ch, rep from * to end, 1 dc to beg ch.

Round 24 1 dc into each of next 8 tr, 4 ch, 1 tr around ch lengths of 2 prev rounds, 4 ch, * 1 dc into each of next 9 tr, 4 ch, 1 tr around ch lengths, 4 ch, rep from * to end, sl st to 1st dc at beg of round.

Round 25 3 ch, 1 tr into each of next 3 dc, (1 tr, 4 ch, 1 tr) into next dc, 1 tr into each of next 4 dc, 7 ch, * 1 tr into each of next 4 dc, (1 tr, 4 ch, 1 tr) into next dc, 1 tr into each of next 4 dc, 7 ch, rep from * to end, sl st to beg ch.

Rounds 26 to 28 Rep rounds 23 to 25, thus completing the 9th set of bells.

Rounds 29 to 46 Cont working in pattern, repeating rounds 23 to 25 in contrasting colour for the 10th, 12th, 13th and 15th bell rows and in main colour for the 11th and 14th bell rows.

Rounds 47 and 48 Using main colour rep rounds 23 and 24. Fasten off.

Bodice

Note: The bodice is worked up from the waist.

With right side facing, insert hook in last of comm.ch of skirt and make 3 ch.

Row 1 Miss 3 tr, (2 tr, 2 ch, 2 tr) into 1st sp between 4 tr groups, * miss 4 tr, (1 tr, 2 ch, 1 tr) (this is a "V") into next sp, miss 4 tr, (2 tr, 2 ch, 2 tr) into next sp, rep from * to last 4 tr, miss 3 tr, 1 tr into last tr, turn.

Row 2 3 ch, (1 tr, 2 ch, 1 tr) into ch sp between next 2 tr groups (the "shells"), (2 tr, 2 ch, 2 tr) in V, rep from * to last shell, (1 tr, 2 ch, 1 tr) into shell, 1 tr into turning ch.

Rows 3 to 9 3 ch, (2 tr, 2 ch, 2 tr) in each V, (1 tr, 2 ch, 1 tr) in each shell, leaving opening for zip fastener. Sl st the two ends of row 9 together and cont to work again in rounds instead of rows.

Round 10 Sl st into each of next 2 tr, sl st into 2 ch sp, (5 ch, 1 tr) in same sp, * shell in next V, V in next shell, rep from * ending 1 shell in open sp at left side opening of bodice, sl st to 3rd ch at beg of round, sl st into space of V.

Round 11 3 ch, (1 tr, 2 ch, 2 tr) in V sp, (same sp as sl st) cont V and shell patt to end, sl st to 3rd beg ch, sl st to next tr, sl st to 2 ch sp of shell.

Round 12 (5 ch, 1 tr) into same sp as sl st, work shells and V's to end, sl st to 3rd ch in beg, sl st to V, sl st to V-sp.

Round 13 3 ch, (1 tr, 2 ch, 2 tr) into same sp as sl st, * 1 ch, 1 V, 1 ch, 1 shell, rep from * to end (thus incr 1 ch between each V and shell), sl st to 3rd beg ch, sl st into next tr, sl st into next sp.

Round 14 (5 ch, 1 tr) into same sp as sl st, * 1 ch, 1 shell, 1 ch, 1 V, rep from * to end, sl st to 3rd ch in V at beg of round.

Rounds 15 to 20 Rep rounds 13 and 14 three times.

Row 21 Armhole decrease Start decr for front armhole above the side opening. After joining round with sl st, work 2 dc into V, 1 dc into 1st tr of next shell, 3 ch, 1 V into same shell, 1 ch, 1 shell into next V, (1 ch,

47

1 shell, 1 ch, 1 V make a complete pattern). Cont until 8 patterns have been worked, 1 tr into next shell, turn.
Rows 22 to 26 3 ch, work 8 patterns, 1 tr into turning ch.

Left shoulder
Row 27 3 ch, 1 V, 1 ch, 1 shell, 1 ch, 1 V, 1 ch, 1 shell, 1 tr into next shell, turn.
Row 28 3 ch, 1 V, 1 shell, 1 V, 1 shell, 1 tr to upper turning ch, (omit 1 ch sps).
Row 29 3 ch, 1 V, 1 shell, 1 V, 2 tr into next V.
Row 30 3 ch, 1 shell into next V, 1 V into next shell, 1 shell into next V, 1 tr into turning ch.
Row 31 3 ch, V into shell, shell into V, V into shell, 1 tr into turning ch.
Rows 32 to 36 As rows 30 and 31. Fasten off.

Right shoulder
Row 27 Insert hook into 3rd V from the left side of work, 3 ch into this V, 1 V into next shell, 1 ch, 1 shell into next V, 1 ch, 1 V, 1 ch, 1 shell, 1 tr into turning ch.
Row 28 3 ch, 1 V, 1 shell, 1 V, 2 tr into V, 1 tr into turning ch.
Row 29 3 ch, 1 tr into sp between ch and 2 tr, 1 shell into next V, 1 V, 1 shell, 1 tr into turning ch.
Row 30 3 ch, 1 V into next shell, 1 shell, 1 V, 1 tr into last ch lp.
Row 31 3 ch, 1 shell, 1 V, 1 shell, 1 tr into turning ch.
Rows 32 to 36 As rows 30 and 31. Fasten off.

Back
Turn work so that the opening for

zip fastener is on your left side; beg work on the right side.
Row 21 Counting from front miss (½ shell, 1 V, ½ shell), work (1 dc, 3 ch) into ch sp of same shell, 1 ch, 1 shell into V, 1 ch, 1 V into shell, complete 8 full patterns, 1 tr into next V.
Row 22 3 ch, * 1 shell into next V, 1 ch, 1 V, 1 ch, rep patt from * to end, 1 tr into turning ch.
Row 23 3 ch, * 1 shell into next V, 1 ch, 1 V, 1 ch, rep from * to end, 1 tr into turning ch.
Rows 24 to 28 As rows 22 and 23, omitting 1 ch sp on 28th row.

Right shoulder
Row 29 3 ch, 1 shell into V, 1 V into next shell, 1 shell into next V, 1 tr into next shell (turn).
Row 30 3 ch, 1 V into shell, 1 shell into V, 1 V into shell, 1 tr into turning ch.
Rows 31 to 36 As rows 29 and 30. Fasten off.

Left shoulder
Row 29 Counting from the left side of work (1 dc, 3 ch) into 2nd V, 1 V into next shell, 1 shell into next V, 1 V into next shell, 1 tr into turning ch.
Rows 30 to 36 As rows 29 and 30 of right shoulder.
Fasten off.

To make up
Join front and back shoulders neatly with dc stitches.

Neck and armhole edging
Row 1 With the right side facing you, work 1 row of dc all round.

Row 2 Work (3 dc, 1 picot) all round.
Picot: 3 ch, sl st to 1st ch.
Work a row of dc round the *side opening,* then sew in the zip fastener.

Additional sizes

	Measurements	No. of foundation ch
Woman	61 cm/24 in waist	163
	66 cm/26 in waist	172
	71 cm/28 in waist	181

For the back and front bodice:

81 cm/32 in bust	7 full patterns across shoulders
86 cm/34 in bust	8 full patterns across shoulders
91 cm/36 in bust	9 full patterns across shoulders

For a 10-12-year-old girl (76 cm/30 in bust), follow instructions for pattern using 5 ply wool and hook 2.00 (old no. 14).

Colour illustration opp.   p. 54.

CABLE PATTERNS

TREBLE-AROUND-TREBLE AND CABLE PATTERNS

Notes and abbreviations

(a) The cable side (cs) is the front of the work or the right side; this is the only side where the cables stand out of the texture. When the cable side is facing away from you, work the double trebles from the wrong side. The double trebles are worked around trebles or double trebles only at the cs.

(b) cr tr — crossed treble
     a f — across front (worked at the cable side)
     a b — across back (worked at the cable side)

(Working from right side of cable pattern)

(Working from wrong side of cable pattern)

DOUBLE CROCHET AND TREBLE-AROUND-TREBLE RIB PATTERN

This exercise and the following treble-around-treble pattern exercise serve as an introduction to the more advanced crochet cable patterns.

Worked over an even number of chain.

Make 26 ch.
Row 1 1 dc into 2nd ch from hook, * 1 tr into next ch, 1 dc into next ch, rep from * to end.
Row 2 1 ch, 1 dc into last worked dc in prev row, * 1 tr around next tr worked from the front (the right side or cable side facing you), 1 dc into next dc, rep from * to end.
Row 3 1 ch, 1 dc into last worked dc in prev row, * 1 tr around next tr from the back of work (wrong side), 1 dc into next dc, rep from * to end.
Repeat rows 2 and 3 to required height for pattern.

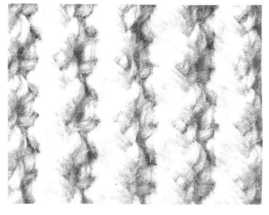

This pattern is very useful for the basque and cuff of crocheted jumpers and cardigans. Treble-around-treble patterns also make attractive ladies'

coats and frocks, or firm fitting
men's jumpers.

A SIMPLE TREBLE-AROUND-TREBLE PATTERN
Note: The cable side is the side of
the work on which the cables stand
out of the texture; this is the right
side.

Worked over multiple of 9 plus 6 ch.

Make 33 ch.
Row 1 1 tr into 4th ch from hook,
1 tr into each ch to end.
Row 2 3 ch, * 1 tr around each of
next 2 tr, 1 tr into each of next
2 tr, 1 tr around each of next 3 tr,
1 tr into each of next 2 tr, rep
from * to last 2 tr, 1 tr around
each of next 2 tr, 1 tr into turning
ch.
Row 3 3 ch, * 1 tr around each of
next 2 tr from cable side, 1 tr into
each of next 2 tr, 1 tr around each
of next 3 tr, 1 tr into each of next
2 tr, rep from * to end, last tr into
turning ch.
Repeat rows 2 and 3 to required
height for pattern.

This pattern may be used for the
same garments as the previous
pattern.

TREBLE-AROUND-TREBLE CROCHET CABLES
In the following instructions the right
side of the cable pattern or the cable
side will be abbreviated as cs.

CABLE PATTERN 1
Make 28 ch.
Row 1 1 tr into 4th ch from hook,
1 tr into each ch to end.
Row 2 (cs row) 3 ch, 1 tr into each
of next 2 tr, miss 1 tr, 1 dtr around
next tr, 1 dtr around missed tr, a f
1 tr into each of next 3 tr, miss 2 tr,
1 dtr around next tr, 1 dtr around
following tr, 1 dtr around 1st missed
tr, bringing hook behind the last
worked 2 dtr (bring the two already
worked dtr downwards with the left
thumb so that the 1st missed tr can
be reached), 1 dtr around 2nd missed
tr working in the same way as for
1st missed tr (this movement will be
referred to as "across back" of the
trebles from now on), miss 2 tr,

1 dtr around each of next 2 tr,
1 dtr around 1st missed tr across
front of dtr's, 1 dtr around next
missed tr across front, 1 tr into each
of next 3 tr, miss 1 tr, 1 dtr around
next tr, 1 dtr around missed tr
across back, miss 1 tr, 1 dtr around
next tr, 1 dtr around missed tr
across front of dtr, 1 tr into each of
last 2 tr, 1 tr into turning ch.

Row 3 3 ch, 1 tr into each of next
2 tr, 1 dtr around next dtr from cs
inserting hook around dtr from back

of row, 1 dtr around each of next 3 dtr from cs, 1 tr into each of next 3 tr, 1 dtr around each of next 8 dtr from cs, 1 tr into each of next 3 tr, 1 dtr around each of next 2 dtr from cs, 1 tr into each of next 2 tr, 1 tr into turning ch.

Row 4 (cs row) 3 ch, 1 tr into each of next 2 tr, miss 1 dtr, 1 dtr around next dtr, 1 dtr around missed dtr, a f 1 tr into each of next 3 tr, miss 2 dtr, 1 dtr around each of next 2 dtr, 1 dtr around 1st missed dtr across back, 1 dtr around 2nd missed dtr across back, miss 2 dtr, 1 dtr around each of next 2 dtr, 1 dtr around 1st missed dtr across front, 1 dtr around 2nd missed dtr across front, 1 tr into each of next 3 tr, miss 1 dtr, 1 dtr around next dtr, 1 dtr around missed dtr across back, miss 1 dtr, 1 dtr around next dtr, 1 dtr around missed dtr across front, 1 tr into each of last 2 tr, 1 tr into turning ch.

Rows 5 to 12 As rows 3 and 4.

CABLE PATTERN 2
Make 32 ch.
Row 1 1 tr into 4th ch from hook, 1 tr into each ch to end.

Row 2 3 ch, 1 tr into each of next 3 tr, miss 2 tr, 1 dtr around next tr, 1 tr into 2nd missed tr across back, 1 ttr around 1st missed tr across front, 1 tr into each of next 3 tr, 1 dtr around next tr, 1 tr into each of next 3 tr, 1 dtr around next tr, 1 tr into each of next 3 tr, miss 2 tr, 1 dtr around each of next 2 tr, 1 dtr around 1st missed tr across front, 1 dtr around 2nd missed tr across front, miss 2 tr, 1 dtr around each of next 2 tr, 1 dtr around 1st missed tr across back, 1 dtr around 2nd missed tr across back, 1 tr into each of next 3 tr, 1 tr into turning ch.

Row 3 3 ch, 1 tr into each of next 3 tr, 1 dtr around each of next 8 dtr inserting hook around the dtr from cs (cable side) of the work leaving every pair of upper threads of these 8 double trebles in prev row in the front of the work (facing you), 1 tr into each of next 3 tr, 1 dtr around next dtr from cs, 1 tr into each of next 3 tr, 1 dtr around next dtr from cs, 1 tr into each of next 3 tr, 1 dtr around next ttr, 1 tr into next tr, 1 dtr around next dtr, 1 tr into each of next 3 tr, 1 tr into turning ch.

Row 4 3 ch, 1 tr into each of next 3 tr, miss (1 dtr, 1 tr), 1 dtr around next dtr, 1 tr into missed tr across back, 1 ttr around missed dtr across front, 1 tr into each of next 3 tr, miss 1 dtr, 1 tr into next tr, 1 dtr around missed dtr across front, 1 tr into next tr, miss 1 tr, 1 dtr around next dtr, 1 tr into missed tr across back, 1 tr into each of next 3 tr, miss 2 dtr, 1 dtr around each of

next 2 dtr, 1 dtr around 1st missed dtr across back, 1 dtr around 2nd missed dtr across back, miss 2 dtr, 1 dtr around each of next 2 dtr, 1 dtr around 1st missed dtr across front, 1 dtr around 2nd missed dtr across front, 1 tr into each of next 3 tr, 1 tr into turning ch.

Row 5 3 ch, 1 tr into each of next 3 tr, 1 dtr around each of next 8 dtr from cs, 1 tr into each of next 4 tr, 1 dtr around next dtr, 1 tr into next tr, 1 dtr around next dtr, 1 tr into next 4 tr, 1 dtr around ttr from cs, 1 tr into next tr, 1 dtr around next dtr from cs, 1 tr into each of next 3 tr, 1 tr into turning ch.

Row 6 3 ch, 1 tr into each of next 3 tr, miss (1 dtr, 1 tr), 1 dtr around next dtr, 1 tr into missed tr across back, 1 ttr around missed dtr across front, 1 tr into each of next 4 tr, miss (1 dtr, 1 tr), 1 dtr around next dtr, 1 tr into missed tr across back, 1 dtr around missed dtr across front, 1 tr into each of next 4 tr, miss 2 dtr, 1 dtr around each of next 2 dtr, 1 dtr around 1st missed dtr across front, 1 dtr around 2nd missed dtr across front, miss 2 dtr, 1 dtr around each of next 2 dtr, 1 dtr around 1st missed dtr across back, 1 dtr around 2nd missed dtr across back, 1 tr into each of next 3 tr, 1 tr into turning ch.

Row 7 3 ch, 1 tr into each of next 3 tr, 1 dtr around each of next 8 dtr from cs, 1 tr into each of next 4 tr, 1 dtr around next dtr from cs, 1 tr into next tr, 1 dtr around next dtr from cs, 1 tr into each of next 4 tr, 1 dtr around next ttr from cs,

1 tr into next tr, 1 dtr around next dtr from cs, 1 tr into each of next 3 tr, 1 tr into turning ch.

Row 8 3 ch, 1 tr into each of next 3 tr, miss (1 dtr, 1 tr), 1 dtr around next ttr, 1 tr into missed tr across back, 1 ttr around missed dtr across front, 1 tr into each of next 3 tr, miss 1 tr, 1 dtr around next dtr, 1 tr into missed tr acrosss back, 1 tr into next tr, miss 1 dtr, 1 tr into next tr, 1 dtr around missed dtr across front, 1 tr into each of next 3 tr, miss 2 dtr, 1 dtr around each of next 2 dtr, 1 dtr around 1st missed dtr across back, 1 dtr around 2nd missed dtr across back, miss 2 dtr, 1 dtr around each next 2 dtr, 1 dtr around 1st missed dtr across front, 1 dtr around 2nd missed dtr across front, 1 tr into each of next 3 tr, 1 tr into turning ch.

Row 9 3 ch, 1 tr into each of next 3 tr, 1 dtr around each of next 8 dtr from cs, 1 tr into each of next 3 tr, 1 dtr around next dtr from cs, 1 tr into each of next 3 tr, 1 dtr around next dtr from cs, 1 tr into each of next 3 tr, 1 dtr around next ttr from cs, 1 tr into next tr, 1 dtr around next dtr from cs, 1 tr into each of next 3 tr, 1 tr into turning ch.

Row 10 3 ch, 1 tr into each of next 3 tr, miss (1 dtr, 1 tr), 1 dtr around next dtr, 1 tr into missed tr across back, 1 ttr around missed dtr across front, 1 tr into each of next 3 tr, 1 dtr around next dtr, 1 tr into each of next 3 tr, 1 dtr around next dtr, 1 tr into each of next 3 tr, miss 2 dtr, 1 dtr around each of next 2 dtr, 1 dtr around 1st missed dtr across

front, 1 dtr around 2nd missed dtr across front, miss 2 dtr, 1 dtr around each of next 2 dtr, 1 dtr around 1st missed dtr across back, 1 dtr around 2nd missed dtr across back, 1 tr into each of next 3 tr, 1 tr into turning ch.

CABLE PATTERN 3
Note: The trebles are to be worked *into the next treble* unless instructed otherwise.

Make 37 ch.
Row 1 1 tr into 4th ch from hook, 1 tr into each ch to end.

Row 2 3 ch, 2 tr, miss 1 tr, 1 dtr around next tr, 1 dtr around missed tr across front, 3 tr, miss 2 tr, 1 dtr around each of next 2 tr, 1 dtr around 1st missed tr across back, 1 dtr around 2nd missed tr across back, miss 2 tr, 1 dtr around each of next 2 tr, 1 dtr around 1st missed tr across back, 1 dtr around 2nd missed tr across back, 3 tr, miss 2 tr, 1 dtr around next tr, 1 tr into 1st missed tr across back, 1 tr into

Bell pattern dress (p. 46).

2nd missed tr across back, miss (the dtr just worked and 1 tr), 2 tr, 1 dtr around missed tr across front, 3 tr, miss 1 tr, 1 dtr around next tr, 1 dtr around missed tr across back, miss 1 tr, 1 dtr around next tr, 1 dtr around missed tr across front, 2 tr, 1 tr into turning ch.

Row 3 3 ch, 2 tr, 1 dtr around each of next 4 dtr from cs (cable side), 3 tr, 1 dtr around next dtr from cs, 4 tr, 1 dtr around next dtr from cs, 3 tr, 1 dtr around each of next 8 dtr from cs, 3 tr, miss 1 dtr, 1 dtr around next dtr from cs, 1 dtr around missed dtr from cs crossing in front of dtr just worked, 2 tr, 1 tr into turning ch. .

Row 4 3 ch, 2 tr, miss 1 dtr, 1 dtr around next dtr, 1 dtr around missed dtr across front, 3 tr, * miss 2 dtr, 1 dtr around each of next 2 dtr, 1 dtr around 1st missed dtr across front, 1 dtr around 2nd missed dtr across front, rep from * once, 3 tr, 1 dtr around next dtr, 4 tr, 1 dtr around next dtr, 3 tr, miss 1 dtr, 1 dtr around next dtr, 1 dtr around missed dtr across back, miss 1 dtr, 1 dtr around next dtr, 1 dtr around missed dtr across front, 2 tr, 1 tr into turning ch.

Row 5 3 ch, 2 tr, 1 dtr around each of next 4 dtr from cs, 3 tr, 1 dtr around next dtr from cs, 4 tr, 1 dtr around next dtr from cs, 3 tr, 1 dtr around each of next 8 dtr from cs, 3 tr, miss 1 dtr, 1 dtr around next dtr from cs, 1 dtr around missed dtr from cs crossing in front of dtr just worked, 2 tr, 1 tr into turning ch.

Row 6 3 ch, 2 tr, miss 1 dtr, 1 dtr around next dtr, 1 dtr around missed

dtr across front, 3 tr, * miss 2 dtr, 1 dtr around each of next 2 dtr, 1 dtr around 1st missed dtr across back, 1 dtr around 2nd missed dtr across back, rep from * once, 3 tr, miss 1 dtr, 2 tr, 1 dtr around missed dtr across front, miss 2 tr, 1 dtr around next dtr, 1 tr into 1st missed tr across back, 1 tr into 2nd missed tr across back, 3 tr, miss 1 dtr, 1 dtr around next dtr, 1 dtr around missed dtr across back, miss 1 dtr, 1 dtr around next dtr, 1 dtr around missed dtr across front, 2 tr, 1 tr into turning ch.

Row 7 3 ch, 2 tr, 1 dtr around each of next 4 dtr from cs, 5 tr, miss 1 dtr, 1 dtr around next dtr from cs, 1 dtr around missed dtr from cs crossing in front of dtr just worked, 1 tr into each of next 5 tr, (make sure you do not work into the dtr), 1 dtr around each of next 8 dtr from cs, 3 tr, miss 1 dtr, 1 dtr around next dtr from cs, 1 dtr around missed dtr from cs crossing in front of dtr just worked, 2 tr, 1 tr into turning ch.

Row 8 3 ch, 2 tr, miss 1 dtr, 1 dtr around next dtr, 1 dtr around missed dtr across front, 3 tr, * miss 2 dtr, 1 dtr around each of next 2 dtr, 1 dtr around 1st missed dtr across front, 1 dtr around 2nd missed dtr across front, rep from * once, 3 tr, miss 2 tr, 1 dtr around next dtr, 1 tr into 1st missed tr across back, 1 tr into 2nd missed tr across back, miss 1 dtr, 2 tr, 1 dtr around missed dtr across front, 3 tr, miss 1 dtr, 1 dtr around next dtr, 1 dtr around missed dtr across back, miss 1 dtr, 1 dtr around next dtr, 1 dtr around missed dtr across front, 2 tr, 1 tr into turning ch.

Row 9 3 ch, 2 tr, 1 dtr around each of next 4 dtr from cs, 3 tr, 1 dtr around next dtr from cs, 4 tr, 1 dtr around next dtr from cs, 3 tr, 1 dtr around each of next 8 dtr from cs, 3 tr, miss 1 dtr, 1 dtr around next dtr from cs, 1 dtr around missed dtr from cs crossing in front of dtr just worked, 2 tr, 1 tr into turning ch.

Row 10 3 ch, 2 tr, miss 1 dtr, 1 dtr around next dtr, 1 dtr around missed dtr across front, 3 tr, * miss 2 dtr, 1 dtr around each of next 2 dtr, 1 dtr around 1st missed dtr across back, 1 dtr around 2nd missed dtr across back, rep from * once, 3 tr, 1 dtr around next dtr, 1 tr into each of next 4 tr, 1 dtr around next dtr, 3 tr, miss 1 dtr, 1 dtr around next dtr, 1 dtr around missed dtr across back, miss 1 dtr, 1 dtr around next dtr, 1 dtr around missed dtr across front, 2 tr, 1 tr into turning ch.

Row 11 As row 9.

Row 12 3 ch, 2 tr, miss 1 dtr, 1 dtr around next dtr, 1 dtr around missed dtr across front, 3 tr, * miss 2 dtr, 1 dtr around each of next 2 dtr, 1 dtr around 1st missed dtr across front, 1 dtr around 2nd missed dtr across front, rep from * once, 3 tr, miss 1 dtr, 2 tr, 1 dtr around missed dtr across front, miss 2 tr, 1 dtr around next dtr, 1 tr into 1st missed tr across back, 1 tr into 2nd missed tr across back, 3 tr, miss 1 dtr, 1 dtr around next dtr, 1 dtr around missed dtr across back, miss 1 dtr, 1 dtr around next dtr, 1 dtr around missed dtr across front, 2 tr, 1 tr into turning ch.

WOMEN'S ARAN CROCHET SKI JUMPER

(Award-winning design: 1st prize, Sydney Royal Easter Show 1973; Ladies' Cardigan and Jumper Exhibition)

Materials

12 ply sportswool or crepe wool: 1150 g (2 lb 8 oz).
Hook 4.50 (no. 7).

Measurements

92 cm (36 in) to fit 86-89 cm (34-35 in) bust;
46 cm (18 in) sleeve;
64 cm (25 in) full length.
For other sizes please see note at the end of the pattern.

Tension: 8 treble to 5 cm (2 in); 4 rows to 5 cm (2 in).

BACK

Make 65 ch.

Row 1 1 tr into 4th ch from hook, 1 tr into each ch to end. (63 tr)

Row 2 3 ch, * 1 dtr around next tr at the back of work, 1 tr into next tr, rep from * to end, last tr into turning ch.

Row 3 3 ch, * 1 dtr around next dtr from cs front, 1 tr into next tr, rep from * to end, last tr into turning ch.

Row 4 3 ch, * 1 dtr around next dtr at the back, 1 tr into next tr, rep from * to end, last tr into turning ch.

Rows 5 to 7 As rows 3-4-3.

Row 8 3 ch, 1 tr into each tr and dtr to end, last tr into turning ch.

Row 9 3 ch, 1 incr tr (work incr tr into tr worked last in prev row — 64 st in row), 1 tr into each of next 3 tr, miss 1 tr, 1 dtr around next tr, 1 dtr around missed tr a b of dtr from cs, miss 1 tr, 1 dtr around next tr, 1 dtr around missed tr a ·f, 1 tr into each of next 4 tr, miss 2 tr, 1 dtr around next tr, 1 tr into

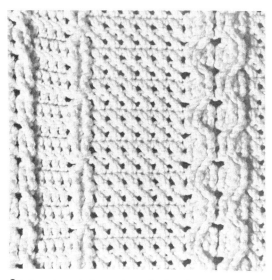

2nd missed tr a b of dtr just worked, 1 dtr around 1st missed tr a f, 6 cr tr (Crossed treble: miss 1 tr, 1 tr into next tr, 1 tr into

missed tr a b of tr just worked — worked the same way on the right and wrong sides of garment), miss 2 tr, 1 dtr around each of next 2 tr, 1 dtr around 1st missed tr a b, 1 dtr around 2nd missed tr a b, miss 2 tr, 1 dtr around each of next 2 tr, 1 dtr around 1st missed tr a f, 1 dtr around 2nd missed tr a f, 6 cr tr, miss 2 tr, 1 dtr around next tr, 1 tr into 2nd missed tr a b of dtr just worked, 1 dtr around 1st missed tr a f, 1 tr into each of next 4 tr, miss 1 tr, 1 dtr around next tr, 1 dtr around missed tr a b of dtr, miss 1 tr, 1 dtr around next tr, 1 dtr around missed tr a f, 1 tr into each of next 4 tr, 1 tr into turning ch.

Row 10 3 ch, 1 incr tr (into tr last worked in prev row), 1 tr into each of next 4 tr, 1 dtr around each of next 4 dtr, 1 tr into each of next 4 tr, 1 dtr around next dtr, 1 tr into next tr, 1 dtr around next dtr, 6 cr tr, 1 dtr around each of next 8 dtr from cs, 6 cr tr, 1 dtr around next dtr, 1 tr into next tr, 1 dtr around next dtr, 1 tr into each of next 4 tr, 1 dtr around each of next 4 dtr, 1 tr into each of next 4 tr, 2 tr into turning ch.

Row 11 3 ch, 1 tr into each of next 5 tr, miss 1 dtr, 1 dtr around next dtr, 1 dtr around missed dtr a b, miss 1 dtr, 1 dtr around next dtr, 1 dtr around missed dtr a f, 1 tr into each of next 4 tr, 1 dtr around next dtr, 1 tr into next tr, 1 dtr around next dtr, 6 cr tr, miss 2 dtr, 1 dtr around each of next 2 dtr, 1 dtr around 1st missed dtr a f, 1 dtr around 2nd missed dtr a f, miss 2 dtr, 1 dtr around each of next 2 dtr, 1 dtr around 1st missed dtr a b, 1 dtr around 2nd missed dtr a b, 6 cr tr, 1 dtr around next dtr, 1 tr into next tr, 1 dtr around next dtr, 1 tr into each of next 4 tr, miss 1 dtr, 1 dtr around next dtr, 1 dtr around missed dtr a b, miss 1 dtr, 1 dtr around next dtr, 1 dtr around missed dtr a f, 1 tr into each of next 5 tr, 1 tr into turning ch.

Row 12 3 ch, 1 tr incr, 1 tr into each of next 5 tr, 1 dtr around each of next 4 dtr, 1 tr into each of next 4 tr, 1 dtr around next dtr, 1 tr into next tr, 1 dtr around next dtr, 6 cr tr, 1 dtr around each of next 8 dtr, 6 cr tr, 1 dtr around next dtr, 1 tr into next tr, 1 dtr around next dtr, 1 tr into each of next 4 tr, 1 dtr around each of next 4 dtr, 1 tr into each of next 5 tr, 2 tr into turning ch.

Row 13 3 ch, 1 incr tr, 1 tr into each of next 6 tr, miss 1 dtr, 1 dtr around next dtr, 1 dtr around missed dtr a b, miss 1 dtr, 1 dtr around next dtr, 1 dtr around missed dtr a f, 1 tr into each of next 4 tr, miss (1 dtr 1 tr), 1 dtr around next dtr, 1 tr into missed tr a b of dtr just worked, 1 dtr around missed dtr a f, 6 cr tr, miss 2 dtr, 1 dtr around each of next 2 dtr, 1 dtr around 1st missed dtr a b, 1 dtr around 2nd missed dtr a b, miss 2 dtr, 1 dtr around each of next 2 dtr, 1 dtr around 1st missed dtr a f, 1 dtr around 2nd missed dtr a f, 6 cr tr, miss (1 dtr, 1 tr), 1 dtr around next dtr, 1 tr into missed tr a b of dtr just worked, 1 dtr around missed dtr

a f, 1 tr into each of next 4 tr, miss 1 dtr, 1 dtr around next dtr, 1 dtr around missed dtr a b, miss 1 dtr, 1 dtr around next dtr, 1 dtr around missed dtr a f, 1 tr into each of next 6 tr, 2 tr into turning ch.
Rows 14 to 33 Work patt as rows 10 to 13 but incr 1 tr each side only in 21st row. (In row 33 there should be 9 tr on both sides.)
Row 34 As row 10 with 9 tr each end.
Row 35 Armhole shaping.
Sl st into each of next 5 tr, 3 ch, 1 decr tr, 2 tr, cont patt as for row 11 from cable onwards to after last cable, 2 tr, 1 decr tr, 1 tr, turn.
* Cont in patt, dec 1 st each end of next 3 rows, then work 4th row without dec. * Rep from * to * to end of row 52.
Fasten off.

FRONT
Work same as for back up to and incl row 47.
Row 48 Left shoulder and neck shaping.
3 ch, 1 decr tr, patt until 4 cr tr have been worked, turn. Cont armhole shaping as before *at the same time* dec 2 sts at neck edge every row to end of row 51.
Row 52 3 ch, 2 decr tr leaving last loops of the trebles on hook, 1 tr, into turning ch leaving last lp on hook, yoh, draw through all loops as in a cluster.
Row 48 Right shoulder and neck.
Count from the centre cable outwards (towards left): miss (centre cable and 2 cr tr), (3 ch, 1 tr) into next cr tr, patt to last 3 sts, 1 decr

tr, 1 tr into turning ch. Complete as left side, reversing all shapings.

SLEEVES
Make 33 ch.

Row 1 1 tr into 4th ch from hook, 1 tr into each ch to end.

Row 2 3 ch, * 1 dtr around next tr (inserting hook on the wrong side of work), 1 tr into next tr, rep from * to end, last tr into turning ch.

Row 3 3 ch, * 1 dtr around next dtr, 1 tr into next tr, rep from * to end, last tr into turning ch.

Row 4 3 ch, * 1 dtr, around next dtr a b, 1 tr into next tr, rep from * to end, last tr into turning ch.

Rows 5 to 7 As rows 3-4-3.

Row 8 3 ch, 1 incr tr, 15 tr, 1 incr tr, 15 tr, 1 incr tr, last tr into turning ch (34 tr).

Row 9 3 ch, 1 incr tr (into tr worked last in prev row), miss 1 tr, 1 dtr around next tr, 1 dtr around missed tr a b, miss 1 tr, 1 dtr around next tr, 1 dtr around missed tr a f, 4 cr tr, miss 2 tr, 1 dtr around each of next 2 tr, 1 dtr around 1st missed tr a b, 1 dtr around 2nd missed tr a b, miss 2 tr, 1 dtr around each of next 2 tr, 1 dtr around 1st missed tr a f, 1 dtr around 2nd missed tr a f, 4 cr tr, miss 1 tr, 1 dtr around next tr, 1 dtr around missed tr a b, miss 1 tr, 1 dtr around next tr, 1 dtr around missed tr a f, 2 tr into turning ch.

Row 10 3 ch, 2 tr into next tr, * 1 dtr around each of next 4 dtr, 4 cr tr, 1 dtr around each of next 8 dtr, 4 cr tr, 1 dtr around each of next 4 dtr *, 2 tr into next tr, 1 tr into turning ch.

Row 11 3 ch, 1 incr tr, 2 tr, * miss 1 dtr, 1 dtr around next dtr, 1 dtr around missed dtr a b, miss 1 dtr, 1 dtr around next dtr, 1 dtr around missed dtr a f, 4 cr tr, miss 2 dtr, 1 dtr around each of next 2 dtr, 1 dtr around 1st missed dtr a f, 1 dtr around 2nd missed dtr a f, miss 2 dtr, 1 dtr around each of next 2 dtr, 1 dtr around 1st missed dtr a b, 1 dtr around 2nd missed dtr a b, 4 cr tr, miss 1 dtr, 1 dtr around next dtr, 1 dtr around missed dtr a b, miss 1 dtr, 1 dtr around next dtr, 1 dtr around missed dtr a f *, 2 tr, 1 incr tr, 1 tr into turning ch.

Row 12 3 ch, 1 tr into each of next 3 tr, * 1 dtr around each of next 4 dtr, 4 cr tr, 1 dtr around each of next 8 dtr, 4 cr tr, 1 dtr around each of next 4 dtr, *3 tr, 1 tr into turning ch.

Row 13 3 ch, 3 tr, * miss 1 dtr, 1 dtr around next dtr, 1 dtr around missed dtr a b, miss 1 dtr, 1 dtr around next dtr, 1 dtr around missed dtr a f, 4 cr tr, miss 2 dtr, 1 dtr around each of next 2 dtr, 1 dtr around 1st missed dtr a b, 1 dtr around 2nd missed dtr a b, miss 2 dtr, 1 dtr around each of next 2 dtr, 1 dtr around 1st missed dtr a f, 1 dtr around 2nd missed dtr a f, 4 cr tr, miss 1 dtr, 1 dtr around next dtr, 1 dtr around missed dtr a b, miss 1 dtr, 1 dtr around next dtr, 1 dtr around missed dtr a f *, 3 tr, 1 tr into turning ch.

Rows 14 to 16 As rows 10, 11 and 12 but incr 1 tr at each end in rows 14 and 16 (6 side tr in row 16).

Rows 17 to 36 Increase 1 tr in every 5th row at each end, patt as for rows 13, 10, 11 and 12 * to * (10 tr each end in row 36).

Row 37 Armhole shaping.
Sl st into each of next 5 tr, 3 ch, 1 decr tr, 1 tr into each of next 3 tr, cont patt as * to * in row 13 to end of last cable, 1 tr into each of next 3 tr, 1 decr tr, turn.

Rows 38 to 52 3 ch, 1 decr st (tr or dtr) in every row at each end, cable pattern as in rows 10-11-12-13; in row 52 you should have only the 8 dtr of the middle cable left. Fasten off.

To make up
Using the same hook and yarn as before and working in dc, join raglan, side and sleeve seams.

POLO NECK
Round 1 Work 1 round of 86 dc from the right side around the neck opening, do not turn.

Round 2 3 ch, * 1 tr into each of next 3 dc, 1 decr tr, rep from * to end, sl st into beg ch (do not turn).

Round 3 3 ch, * 1 tr into each of next 4 tr, 1 decr tr, rep from * to end, sl st into beg ch, turn (58 tr).

Round 4 (working from the inside of garment): 3 ch, * 1 dtr around next tr, 1 tr into next tr, rep from * to end, sl st into beg ch, do not turn work for this or for the foll rounds.

Round 5 3 ch, * 1 dtr around next dtr, 1 tr into next tr, rep from * to end, sl st into beg ch.

Rounds 6 to 12 As round 5.
Fold collar in half to right side.

Colour illustration opp. p. 55.

Note: Working the same design for children's jumper: 66 cm (26 in) chest for 9-11-year-old: use 8 ply wool working with a 3.50 (no. 9) hook; tension 5 tr to 2.5 cm (1 in). For a 56 cm (22 in) chest for small child: use 5 ply wool and a 2.50 (no. 12) hook; tension 6 tr to 2.5 cm (1 in).
The pattern description as above can then be followed.

MAN'S ARAN CROCHET SKI JUMPER
Note: For explanations and abbreviations please see the notes before "Women's Aran Crochet Ski Jumper". Crossed treble (cr tr): miss 1 tr, 1 tr into next tr, 1 tr into missed tr across back of tr just worked -- to work the same way on the right and wrong sides of garment.

Materials
12 ply sportswool or crepe wool: 1200 g (2 lb 11 oz). If you use a light colour the cables will show up much better.
Hook 4.50 (no. 7).

Measurements
96 cm (38 in) to fit 91-94 cm (36-37 in) chest
50 cm (19½ in) sleeve
70 cm (27½ in) full length
For sizes other than given here please see note at the end of this pattern.

Tension: 8 tr to 5 cm (2 in); 4 rows to 5 cm (2 in).

FRONT
Make 69 ch.

Row 1 1st tr into 4th ch from hook, 1 tr into each ch to end (67 tr).

Row 2 3 ch, * 1 dtr around next tr, 1 tr into next tr, rep from * to end, last tr into turning ch.

Row 3 3 ch, * 1 dtr around next dtr from cs, 1 tr into next tr, rep from * to end, last tr into turning ch.

Row 4 3 ch, * 1 dtr around next dtr, 1 tr into next tr, rep from * to end, last tr into turning ch.

Row 5 Increase row: 3 ch, 1 tr into each st (tr and dtr) of row with incr 1 tr each end and 1 tr in the centre (70 tr), last tr into turning ch.

Row 6 3 ch, 4 cr tr, miss 2 tr, 1 dtr around each of next 2 tr, 1 dtr around 1st missed tr a f, 1 dtr around 2nd missed tr a f, 1 tr into each of next 4 tr, 1 dtr around each of next 2 tr, 1 tr into each of next 2 tr, 1 dtr around each of next 2 tr, 4 cr tr, miss 2 tr, 1 dtr around each

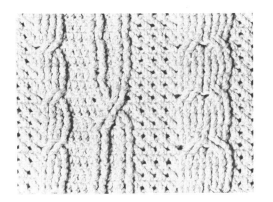

of next 2 tr, 1 dtr around 1st missed tr a b, 1 dtr around 2nd missed tr a b, miss 2 tr, 1 dtr around each of next 2 tr, 1 dtr around 1st missed tr a f, 1 dtr around 2nd missed tr a f, 4 cr tr,

1 dtr around each of next 2 tr.

1 tr into each of next 2 tr, 1 dtr around each of next 2 tr, 1 tr into each of next 4 tr, miss 2 tr, 1 dtr around each of next 2 tr, 1 dtr around 1st missed tr a f, 1 dtr around 2nd missed tr a f, 4 cr tr, 1 tr into turning ch.

Row 7 3 ch, 4 cr tr, 1 dtr around each of next 4 dtr, 1 tr into each of next 4 tr, 1 dtr around each of next 2 dtr, 1 tr into each of next 2 tr, 1 dtr around each of next 2 dtr, 4 cr tr, 1 dtr around each of next 8 dtr, 4 cr tr, 1 dtr around each of next 2 dtr, 1 tr into each of next 2 dtr, 1 tr into each of next 4 tr, 1 dtr around each of next 4 dtr, 4 cr tr, 1 tr into turning ch.

Row 8 As row 7.

Row 9 As row 7.

Row 10 3 ch, 4 cr tr, miss 2 dtr, 1 dtr around each of next 2 dtr, 1 dtr around 1st missed dtr a f, 1 dtr around 2nd missed dtr a f, 1 tr into each of next 4 tr, 1 dtr around each of next 2 dtr, 1 tr into each of next 2 tr, 1 dtr around each of next 2 dtr, 4 cr tr, miss 2 dtr, 1 dtr around each of next 2 dtr, 1 dtr around 1st missed dtr a b, 1 dtr around 2nd missed dtr a b, miss 2 dtr, 1 dtr around each of next 2 dtr, 1 dtr around 1st missed dtr a f, 1 dtr around 2nd missed dtr a f, 4 cr tr, 1 dtr around each of next 2 dtr, 1 tr into each of next 2 tr, 1 dtr around each of next 2 dtr, 1 tr into each of next 4 tr, miss 2 dtr, 1 dtr around each of next 2 dtr, 1 dtr around 1st missed dtr a f, 1 dtr around 2nd missed dtr a f, 4 cr tr, 1 tr into turning ch.

Row 11 As row 7.

Row 12 As row 8.

Row 13 Increase row: As row 7 but incr 1 tr at each end.

Row 14 3 ch, 1 tr into next tr, 1 tr into tr worked last in prev row working a b of tr just worked, 4 cr tr, miss 2 dtr, 1 dtr around each of next 2 dtr, 1 dtr around 1st missed dtr a f, 1 dtr around 2nd missed dtr a f, 1 tr into each of next 4 tr, miss 2 dtr, 1 tr into next tr, 1 dtr around 1st missed dtr a f, 1 dtr around 2nd missed dtr a f, miss 1 tr, 1 dtr around each of next 2 dtr, 1 tr into missed tr a b of the 2 dtr, 4 cr tr, miss 2 dtr, 1 dtr around each of next 2 dtr, 1 dtr around 1st missed dtr a b, 1 dtr around 2nd missed dtr a b, miss 2 dtr, 1 dtr around each of next 2 dtr, 1 dtr around 1st missed dtr a f, 1 dtr around 2nd missed dtr a. f, 4 cr tr, miss 2 dtr, 1 tr into next tr, 1 dtr around 1st missed dtr a f, 1 dtr around 2nd missed dtr a f, miss 1 tr, 1 dtr around each of next 2 dtr, 1 tr into missed tr a b of the 2 dtr, 1 tr into each of next 4 tr, miss 2 dtr, 1 dtr around each of next 2 dtr, 1 dtr around 1st missed dtr a f, 1 dtr around 2nd missed dtr a f, 4 cr tr, miss 1 tr, 1 tr into turning ch, 1 tr into missed tr a b of tr, 1 tr again in turning ch.

Row 15 3 ch, 5 cr tr, 1 dtr around each of next 4 dtr, 1 tr into each of next 4 tr, 1 tr in next tr, miss 2 dtr, 1 dtr around each of next 2 dtr cs, 1 dtr around first missed dtr, 1 dtr around 2nd missed dtr cs, 1 tr in next tr, 4 cr tr, 1 dtr around each of next 8 dtr, 4 cr tr, 1 tr in next tr, miss 2 dtr, 1 dtr around each of next 2 dtr cs, 1 dtr around first missed dtr, 1 dtr around 2nd missed dtr cs, 1 tr in next tr, 1 tr into each of next 4 tr, 1 dtr around each of next 4 dtr, 5 cr tr, 1 tr in turning ch.

Row 16 3 ch, 5 cr tr, 1 dtr around each of next 4 dtr, 1 tr into each of next 4 tr, miss 1 tr, 1 dtr around each of next 2 dtr, 1 tr into missed tr a b, miss 2 dtr, 1 tr into next tr, 1 dtr around 1st missed dtr a f, 1 dtr around 2nd missed dtr a f, 4 cr tr, 1 dtr around each of next 8 dtr, 4 cr tr, miss 1 tr, 1 dtr around each of next 2 dtr, 1 tr into missed tr a b, miss 2 dtr, 1 tr into next tr, 1 dtr around 1st missed dtr a f, 1 dtr around 2nd missed dtr a f, 1 tr into each of next 4 tr, 1 dtr around each of next 4 dtr, 5 cr tr, 1 tr into turning ch.

Row 17 3 ch, 5 cr tr, 1 dtr around each of next 4 dtr, 1 tr into each of next 4 tr, 1 dtr around each of next 2 dtr, 1 tr into each of next 2 tr, 1 dtr around each of next 2 dtr, 4 cr tr, 1 dtr around each of next 8 dtr, 4 cr tr, 1 dtr around each of next 2 dtr, 1 tr into each of next 2 tr, 1 dtr around each of next 2 dtr, 1 tr into each of next 4 tr, 1 dtr around each of next 4 dtr, 5 cr tr, 1 tr into turning ch.

Row 18 As row 10, but with 5 cr tr each side.

Rows 19 to 30 Cable patterns as rows 7 to 18 with 5 cr tr each side.

Rows 31 to 33 Cable patt as rows 7 to 9 with 5 cr tr each side.

Row 34 Armhole shaping

62

Sl st into next 3 tr, 3 ch, 1 tr into next tr, 3 cr tr, cables as in row 10 to end of last cable, 3 cr tr, 1 tr into each of next 2 tr, turn.

Rows 35 to 42 Decr rows: cables as in rows 11 to 18 but decr 1 st (tr or dtr) at each end of every row for raglan shaping.

Rows 43 to 47 Cont decr 1 st at each end, cable or part cable as in rows 7 to 11.

Shape left shoulder and neck.

Row 48 3 ch, 1 decr tr, 1 dtr around each of next 2 dtr, 2 tr, 1 dtr around each of next 2 dtr, 4 cr tr, 1 decr dtr around the 2 right outside dtr of middle cable, turn.

Row 49 3 ch, 2 decr tr, 1 tr, 2 cr tr, 1 dtr around each of next 2 dtr, 2 tr, 1 dtr around next dtr, 1 dtr decr, 1 tr into turning ch.

Row 50 3 ch, 1 decr, 2 tr, 1 dtr around each of next 2 dtr, 2 cr tr, miss 1 tr, 1 decr tr.

Row 51 3 ch, 2 decr tr, 1 dtr around each of next 2 dtr, 1 tr, 1 decr tr, 1 tr into turning ch.

Row 52 3 ch, 1 decr tr, 1 dtr around next 1 dtr, 2 decr tr.
Fasten off.

Shape right side.

Row 48 1 decr dtr around left outside 2 dtr of middle cable, 4 cr tr, 1 dtr around each of next 2 dtr, 1 tr into each of next 2 tr, 1 dtr around each of next 2 dtr, 1 decr tr, 1 tr into turning ch. Cont as left side reversing shapings.

BACK

Rows 1 to 48 Work same as front.
Rows 49 to 52 Cont working in cable pattern with 1 st (tr or dtr) decr at each end of every row for raglan shaping and omitting neck shaping.

SLEEVES

Make 33 ch.

Row 1 1 tr into 4th ch from hook, 1 tr into each ch to end (31 tr).

Row 2 3 ch, *1 dtr around next tr, 1 tr into next tr, rep from * to end, last tr into turning ch.

Row 3 3 ch, *1 dtr around next dtr, 1 tr into next tr, rep from * to end, last tr into turning ch.

Rows 4 to 6 As row 3.

Row 7 3 ch, 1 tr into each tr and dtr to end and incr 1 tr at beg, 1 tr at centre and 1 tr at end of row (34 tr).

Row 8 3 ch, 1 tr into tr worked last in prev row, 1 tr into next tr, miss 2 tr, 1 dtr around each of next 2 tr, 1 dtr around 1st missed tr a f, 1 dtr around 2nd missed dtr a f, 4 cr tr, 1 dtr around each of next 2 tr, 1 tr into each of next 2 tr, 1 dtr around each of next 2 tr, 4 cr tr, miss 2 tr, 1 dtr around each of next 2 tr, 1 dtr around 1st missed tr a f, 1 dtr around 2nd missed tr a f, 1 tr into next tr, 2 tr into turning ch.

Row 9 3 ch, 1 tr into each of next 2 tr, 1 dtr around each of next 4 dtr, 4 cr tr, 1 dtr around each of next 2 dtr, 1 tr into each of next 2 tr, 1 dtr around each of next 2 dtr, 4 cr tr, 1 dtr around each of next 4 dtr, 1 tr into each of next 2 tr, 1 tr into turning ch.

Row 10 3 ch, 1 tr into each of next 2 tr, 1 dtr around each of next

4 dtr, 4 cr tr, 1 dtr around each of next 2 dtr, 1 tr into each of next 2 tr, 1 dtr around each of next 2 dtr, 4 cr tr, 1 dtr around each of next 4 dtr, 1 tr into each of next 2 tr, 1 tr into turning ch.

Row 11 3 ch, 1 tr into tr worked last in prev row, 1 tr into each of next 2 tr, 1 dtr around each of next 4 dtr, 4 cr tr, 1 dtr around each of next 2 dtr, 1 tr into each of next 2 tr, 1 dtr around each of next 2 dtr, 4 cr tr, 1 dtr around each of next 4 dtr, 1 tr into each of next 2 tr, 2 tr into turning ch.

Row 12 3 ch, 1 tr into each of next 3 tr, miss 2 dtr, 1 dtr around each of next 2 dtr, 1 dtr around 1st missed dtr a f, 1 dtr around 2nd missed dtr a f, 4 cr tr, miss 2 dtr, 1 tr into next tr, 1 dtr around 1st missed dtr a f, 1 dtr around 2nd missed dtr a f, miss 1 tr, 1 dtr around each of next 2 dtr, 1 tr into missed tr a b, 4 cr tr, miss 2 dtr, 1 dtr around each of next 2 dtr, 1 dtr around 1st missed dtr a f, 1 dtr around 2nd missed dtr a f, 1 tr into each of next 3 tr, 1 tr into turning ch.

Cont in front patt as set by these rows, inc 1 st each end of 15th and 17th rows, then every 5th row until there are 10 tr at each side edge. Cont straight to row 38.

Armhole shaping
Row 39 Sl st into each of next 5 tr, 3 ch, 1 decr tr, 3 tr, cable pattern to last 10 tr, 3 tr, 1 decr tr, turn.

Rows 40 to 57 Cont in patt dec 1 st at each end of every row.
Fasten off.

To make up
Using the same yarn and hook as before and working in dc, join raglan, side and sleeve seams.

POLO NECK
Round 1 Work 1 round of dc around neck opening from the right side of the garment.
Round 2 3 ch, 1 tr into each dec of round, sl st to upper beg ch.
Round 3 dec round: 3 ch, work in tr dec evenly to 62 sts, sl st to beg ch.
Round 4 3 ch, *1 dtr around next tr, 1 tr into next tr, rep from * to end, sl st to beg ch, turn and work from the inside of neck.
Round 5 3 ch, *1 dtr around next dtr, 1 tr into next tr, rep from * to end, sl st to beg ch, do not turn.
Round 6 onwards Rep round 5 to required depth of collar (6 to 8 rounds).
Fasten off.
Fold upper part to right side.

Note: Boy's jumper for 66 cm (26 in) chest size:

Materials
8 ply wool; hook 3.50 (no. 9).

Tension: 5 tr to 2.5 cm (1 in); 2 rows to 2.5 cm (1 in).
The pattern description as for the man's jumper can be followed.
Colour illustration opp. p. 70.

PART II

Tricot

INTRODUCTION

Tricot crochet, also known as *Tunisian* or *Afghan stitching*, resembles crocheting, as it is also worked with a hook. However, in common crochet there is only one stitch on the hook at a time — the stitch being worked — even though there may be several loops on the hook as parts of a stitch.

In tricot crochet stitches of the row build up on the hook, as in knitting. Tricot hooks therefore are longer than the corresponding size crochet hooks. The most common sizes are nos. 3.00, 3.50, 4.00, 4.50 and 5.00.

The work starts with a row of chain stitches, and the "chain" is worked exactly the same way as in common crochet. This is followed by the working of the stitches of the foundation row, until the required number has been built up on the hook.

The next step is the completion of the row by the *lock chain*. This means locking off the stitches with a chain-like movement from left to right, working them off the hook stitch by stitch. Notice that I prefer the use of the term "lock chain" to calling it an extra row, as this movement adds no further height to the fabric.

Another distinctive feature of tricot (and also of Lace Tricot) is that it is always worked from the right side and there is no need to turn at the end of the row.

The comprehensive set of patterns which follow includes some exciting new combinations never published before.

The old, known treble stitch is included among the stitches for the sake of completeness. This stitch, however, does not result in a straight-edged texture; the edges slant from the left to the right. Therefore tricot treble of this old style is practically useless. Proper, right-angle edges result by using Lace Tricot, as we will see in Part III of this book.

TRICOT DESIGNS AND BASIC STITCHES

TRICOT DESIGNS AND BASIC STITCHES

It is important to remember when working tricot or Lace Tricot patterns, or designing garments, that the fabric *will not stretch* as will knitted or crocheted ones. Therefore the garments must be designed and worked as tailor-made ones to the correct measurements.

For dresses, a part must be left open at the waist for the zip fastener or for the buttons. The same applies to the opening at the neckline, front or back, when it is worked right up to the collar. As the fabric is firm, ladies' skirts and dresses will not seat when worked using these techniques.

Tricot stitching can also produce neat textures for men's waistcoats and cardigans, children's and baby-wear, decorative articles, such as cushion covers and multi-coloured rugs.

With jumpers it is advisable to knit the basque and sometimes also the neck and the cuff as these parts of the garment are more practical when they stretch a little. A tricot basque can be worked with an opening on the front — a belt-like design — with a buckle.

THE LOCK CHAIN

An instruction for the lock chain may read something like this: "yarn over hook, draw through 2 loops, yarn over hook, draw through 3 loops" and so on.

This can be abbreviated as follows:

"L ch : through 2, through 3 . . . ", meaning yoh, draw through the given number of loops.
"Through 1, through 2, through 1" etc can be further abbreviated as "through 1-2-1".

Please remember that the last loop remaining on the hook from the drawing through movement also counts as the first loop of the next row.

BASIC TRICOT STITCHES

Name of stitch (and commonly used alternative names)	Abbreviation
Tricot double crochet (Tunisian stitch, plain stitch, Afghan stitch)	tc dc (tc pl, pl st)
Tricot treble (Tunisian treble stitch)	tc tr
Purl (tricot purl)	P (tc p)
Knit (tricot knit stitch, Tunisian stocking stitch)	K (tc k, st st)

TRICOT DOUBLE CROCHET

This stitch is comparable in height to the double crochet stitch and is also known as Afghan stitch, Tunisian stitch or plain stitch.

Make 20 ch for a practice piece.
Row 1 Insert hook into 2nd ch from hook, draw 1 lp through leaving it on hook, *insert hook into next ch, draw 1 lp through leaving it on

hook, rep from * into each ch to end of row leaving all remaining loops on hook.

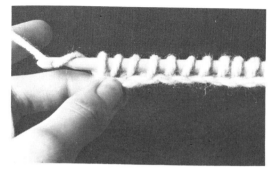

To complete the row lock off the stitches by working the lock chain (L ch) as follows:
* yoh, draw through 2 loops, rep from * until 1 loop is left on hook. This last remaining loop stands for the first stitch of the next row.

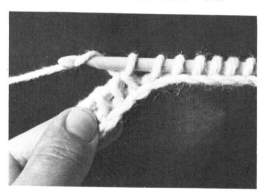

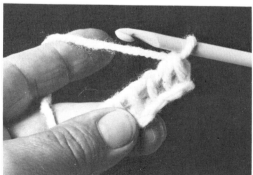

Row 2 You will observe that the front upright half of each stitch stands out of the texture. We shall call this clearly visible loop the *front bar* (f b). This is the part of the stitch we work into.

Don't work into the front bar directly under the remaining loop otherwise you increase 1 stitch. Remember this rule for all tricot patterns.
Insert hook into next f b, draw 1 lp through leaving rem lp on hook, work thus 1 tc dc into each f b to last 2 f b leaving all rem lp on hook. It is important to remember that since these two left-hand stitches were looped together with the lock chain of the preceding row, you have to work separately into both of them in order to retain the correct number of stitches.
Work 2nd last tc dc into next f b,

for last tc dc in row, insert hook into the two outside threads for one stitch as illustrated.

L ch: * yoh, draw through 2 loops, rep from * to end, until 1 lp is left on hook.
Rows 3 to 5 As row 2.

Practise this stitching to perfection, particularly the working of the left edge, as this edging is used in every tricot plain, purl and cross stitch pattern.

As plain tricot is inclined to curl up it is advisable to work tc dc patterns on a foundation row of purl stitches to keep the lower edge straight.

TRICOT PURL STITCH
Make 20 ch.
Row 1 Insert hook into 2nd ch from hook from the *back* of the ch, yoh, draw it through to the back, * bring yarn forward, insert hook into next ch from back, yoh, draw it through ch to the back, rep from * into

70

Man's aran crochet ski jumper (p. 60).

a

b

c

d

each ch leaving all rem lp on hook.
L ch: Through 2 to end.

TRICOT KNIT STITCH
This stitch results in a texture resembling double-knit.

Make 30 ch.
Row 1 (tc dc foundation row) 1 tc dc into 2nd ch from hook, 1 tc dc into each ch to end leaving loops on hook.
L ch: Through 2 to end.
Row 2 (with rem lp on hook) *

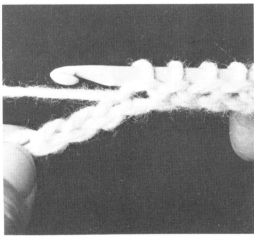

Row 2 Bring yarn in front of hook, miss f b under rem lp, * insert hook into next f b, yoh draw through f b to the back (not to the front otherwise the loop twists), bring yarn to front, * work 1 purl stitch into each f b to last st, as from * to *, 1 tc dc into 2 outside threads of last st (all lp rem on hook).
L ch: Through 2 to end.
Rows 3 to 20 As row 2.

a. Mauve sample: plain and purl combination pattern, tricot (p. 78).
b. Blue sample: honeycomb pattern (moss stitch) (p. 78).
c. Green sample: double row pattern, tricot (p. 76).
d. Orange sample: plain and purl pattern, tricot (p. 76).

insert hook into next lp pushing it right through to the back (under the L ch in prev row and not into the f b), yoh, draw it through, leaving rem lp on hook, rep from * into each st.
L ch: Through 2 to end.

Rows 3 to 14 As row 2.

A very warm fabric may be worked with this stitch for winter-wear, ski jumpers, garments for polar expeditions . . . to mention a few possibilities.

DECREASING AND INCREASING

Simple decreasing and increasing is illustrated on this tc dc exercise; the principle of working two-into-one and one-into-two known from crocheting also applies to the tricot stitches.

Make 20 ch.
Row 1 1 tc dc into 2nd ch from hook, 1 tc dc into each ch to end leaving rem lp on hook.
L ch: Through 2 to end.
Row 2 decr row: rem lp on hook stands for 1st st, insert hook into next f b, yoh, draw it through, insert hook into next 2 f b, yoh, draw through the 2 f b (1 tc dc decreased), 1 tc dc into each f b to 4th last, insert hook into next 2 f b, yoh, draw through the 2 f b (another tc dc decreased), 1 tc dc into each of last 2 f b. (Remember that the 2 outer threads stand for the f b of last st.)
L ch: Through 2 to end.
Continue decreasing 2 tc dc in each row by working together the 3rd and 4th and the 4th last and 3rd last f b until 7 tc dc rem.

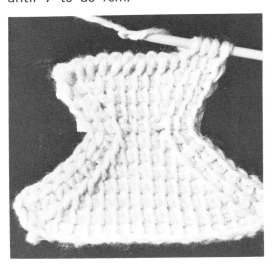

Increase rows: 2 tc dc, insert hook into L ch between 3rd and 4th f b, yoh, draw through, leaving lp on hook, 1 tc dc into each f b to last 4, insert hook into L ch between next 2 f b (4th and 3rd last), yoh, draw through (2 tc dc increased in row), 1 tc dc into each of last 3 f b.
L ch: Through 2 to end.
Increase in every following row until inc to starting width of the sample piece.

EDGE DECREASING
Make 32 ch.
Row 1 1 tc dc into 2nd ch, 1 tc dc into each ch to end.
L ch: Through 2 to end, rem lp stands for 1st st of next row.

Row 2 Miss f b under rem lp, insert hook into next 2 f b, yoh, draw through (1 tc dc decreased).

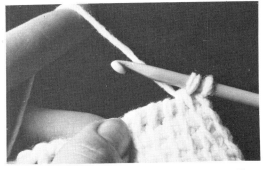

1 tc dc into each f b to last 3 f b, insert hook into next 2 f b, yoh, draw through (another tc dc decreased), last tc dc into 2 outside threads.

L ch: Through 2 to end.

Row 3 Tc dc row without decr.

L ch: Through 2 to end.

Rows 4 to 26 As rows 2 and 3 (decr every 2nd row).

Depending on the required depth of decrease, every 2nd row (as in the exercise) or every 3rd row may be a decrease row. The decr stitches are being worked away from the centre of the piece. This system is thus suitable for dart shaping as well.

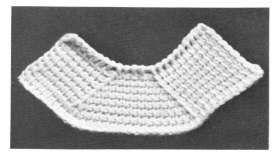

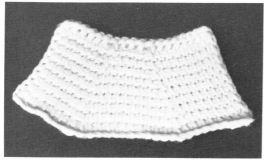

The rule for dart shaping is to leave an equal number of stitches at both sides of the garment and take the decrease stitches away from the inside or centre part.

RAGLAN DECREASE EXERCISES

Raglan decrease 1

Make 21 ch.

Row 1 1 tc dc into 2nd ch, 1 tc dc into each ch to end leaving rem loops on hook.

L ch: Through 2 to end.

Rows 2 to 4 Tc dc rows.

Row 5 Sl st into each of next 5 f b (slip stitch is explained in Part I), 1 P, insert hook into next 2 f b, yoh, draw through (1 tc dc decr), 1 P into next f b, 1 tc dc into each f b to end.

L ch: Through 2 to end.

Row 6 1 P, insert hook into next 2 f b for 1 tc dc decr, 1 P into next f b, 1 tc dc into each f b to end.

L ch: Through 2 to end.

Rows 7 to 10 As row 6.

For raglan decrease of large jumpers or cardigans the decrease rows may be every 2nd or 3rd row working the two sides of the garment correspondingly.

Raglan decrease 2

Make 21 ch.

Rows 1 to 4 As rows 1 to 4 of Raglan decrease (1).

Row 5 Sl st into each of next 5 f b, * 1 tc dc, 1 tc dc decr, 1 tc dc into each rem f b to end.
L ch: Through 2 to end **.
Rows 6 to 10 As row 5 from * to **.
For large garments decrease every 2nd or 3rd row each side.

Raglan decrease 3
Make 27 ch.
Row 1 tc dc row.
Row 2 Sl st into each next 3 f b,

*1 tc dc, 1 tc dc decr, 1 P, 1 tc dc into each rem f b to end.
L ch: Through 2 to end **.
Rows 3 to 12 As row 2 from * to **.

In garments such raglans would be worked up to the shoulder height.

MORE TRICOT STITCHES AND PATTERNS

CROSS STITCH

Make 20 ch.

Row 1 1 tc dc into 2nd ch from hook, 1 tc dc into each ch to end leaving rem loops on hook. (This is your tc dc foundation row.)
L ch: Through 2 to end.

Row 2 Do not count f b under rem lp, * miss next f b, insert hook into following f b, draw 1 lp through, insert hook into missed f b, draw 1 lp through, rep from * to last f b, draw 1 lp through the 2 outside threads of last tc dc.
L ch: Through 2 to end.

Rows 3 to 12 As row 2.

COMBINATION PLAIN AND KNIT STITCH

Worked over an uneven number of ch.

Make 29 ch.

Row 1 Insert hook into 3rd ch from hook, yoh, draw through ch, yoh, draw through the lp on hook leaving it on hook.
(The first draw was a tc dc, the next draw added a knit stitch or chain to the tc dc).
* Insert hook into next ch, yoh, draw it through ch, yoh, draw through lp on hook leaving lp on hook, rep from * into each ch to end leaving rem upper loops on hook.
L ch: Through 2 to end.

Row 2 1 ch, miss f b under ch, * insert hook into next f b, yoh, draw it through f b, yoh, draw through lp on hook leaving this lp on hook, rep from * into each f b to end leaving rem upper loops on hook.
L ch: Through 2 to end.

Rows 3 to 10 As row 2.

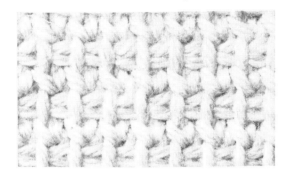

DOUBLE ROW PATTERN

Worked over a ch of multiple of 3 plus 2.

Make 23 ch.

Row 1 1 tc dc into 2nd ch from hook, 1 tc dc into each ch to end leaving loops on hook.
L ch: Through 2 to end.

Row 2 Miss f b under rem lp, 1 tc dc into next f b, *1 P into next f b, 1 tc dc into each of next 2 f b, rep from * to end leaving all loops on hook.
L ch: As for row 1.

Rows 3 to 20 As row 2.

Colour illustration opp. p. 71.

PLAIN AND PURL PATTERN

Worked over a ch of multiple of

76

4 plus 8.

Make 32 ch.
Row 1 1st tc dc into 2nd ch, 1 tc dc into next ch, 1 P into each of next 2 ch, *1 tc dc into each of next 2 ch, 1 P into each of next 2 ch, rep from * to last 3 ch, 1 tc dc into each of last 3 ch.
L ch: Through 2.
Row 2 Miss f b under rem lp, *1 tc dc into each of next 2 f b, 1 P into each of next 2 f b, rep from * to last 3 f b, 1 tc dc into each of next 2 f b, 1 tc dc into 2 outside threads.
L ch: Through 2.
Row 3 *1 P into each of next 2 f b, 1 tc dc into each of next 2 f b, rep from * to last 3 f b, 1 P into each of next 2 f b, 1 tc dc into 2 outside threads.
L ch: Through 2.
Row 4 As row 3.
Rows 5-6 As row 2.
Rows 7-8 As row 3.
Rows 9-10 As row 2.

This pattern gives an excellent combination of stitches and is suitable for many kinds of garments, such as jumpers and cardigans with knitted button-band and buttonhole band.
Colour illustration opp. p. 71.

PLAIN AND PURL SQUARE PATTERN
Worked over a ch of multiple of 8 plus 2.

Make 26 ch.

Row 1 1st tc dc into 2nd ch from hook, 1 tc dc into each of next 3 ch, 1 P into each of next 4 ch, *1 tc dc into each of next 4 ch, 1 P into each of next 4 ch, rep from * to last ch, 1 tc dc into last ch.
L ch: Through 2.
Row 2 Miss f b under rem lp, *1 tc dc into each of next 4 f b, 1 P into each of next 4 f b, rep from * to last st, 1 tc dc into 2 outside threads.
L ch: Through 2.
Rows 3-4 As row 2.
Row 5 Miss f b under rem lp, *1 P into each of next 4 f b, 1 tc dc into each of next 4 f b, rep from * to last st, 1 tc dc into 2 outside threads.
L ch: Through 2.
Rows 6-8 As row 5.
Rows 9-12 As row 2.
Rows 13-16 As row 5.

STRIPE PATTERN IN PLAIN AND PURL STITCHES
Worked over a multiple of 4 plus 1 ch.

Make 41 ch.
Row 1 1 tc dc into 2nd ch, 1 tc dc into each ch to end.
L ch: Through 2.

Row 2 * 1 P into each of next 3
f b, 1 tc dc into next f b, rep from
* to end, last tc dc into 2 outside
threads.
L ch: Through 2.
Row 3 * 1 P into next f b, 1 tc dc
into next f b, rep from * to end,
last tc dc into 2 outside threads.
L ch: Through 2.
Rows 4-5 As row 2.
Row 6 As row 3.
Rows 7 to 18 As rows 4 to 6.

This pattern is suitable for slacks,
suits and for coats. You will notice
that the first row turns upwards; it
is intended to do this, as a decorative
finish on the lower edge of the
garment.

HONEYCOMB PATTERN
(Moss stitch)
Worked over an even number of ch.

Make 22 ch.
Row 1 1st tc dc into 2nd ch, 1 tc
dc into each ch to end.
L ch: Through 2.
Row 2 (1 tc dc, 1 P) to end, last
tc dc into 2 outside threads.
L ch: Through 2.
Row 3 (1 P, 1 tc dc) to end, last
tc dc into 2 outside threads.

78

L ch: Through 2.
Rows 4 to 15 As rows 2 and 3.
Colour illustration opp. p. 71.

PRACTICE PIECE IN DIFFERENT PATTERN ROWS
Worked over an even number of ch,
in purl stitch (P), cross stitch (cr st)
and in tricot double crochet.

Make 44 ch.
Row 1 Insert hook into 2nd ch from
back, yarn under hook, draw yarn
through to the back (purl stitch
made), work 1 P into each ch to
end.
L ch: Through 2.
Row 2 (Do not count f b under lp
on hook), miss 1 f b, 1 tc dc into
next f b, 1 tc dc into missed f b
(cross stitch made), work cr tr to
end, last tc dc into 2 outside threads.
L ch: Through 2.
Row 3 Tc dc row.
L ch: Through 2.
Row 4 P row.
Row 5 Cr st row.

Row 6 Tc dc row.
Row 7 P row.
Row 8 Cr st row.
Row 9 Tc dc row.
Row 10 Finish with P row, l ch:
through 2 as for all rows.

PLAIN AND PURL COMBINATION PATTERN
Worked over a ch of multiple of
4 plus 2.

Make 26 ch.
Row 1 1st tc dc into 2nd ch, * 1 P

into each of next 2 ch, 1 tc dc into next ch, rep from * to end.
L ch: Through 2.

Row 2 (Do not work into f b under rem lp), 1 P into next f b, * 1 tc dc into next f b, 1 P into each of next 2 f b, rep from * to last 3 f b, 1 tc dc into next f b, 1 P into next f b, last tc dc into 2 outside threads.
L ch: Through 2.

Row 3 * 2 P, 1 tc dc, rep from * to end, 1 tc dc into 2 outside threads.
L ch: Through 2.

Row 4 * 1 tc dc, 2 P, rep from * to end, 1tc dc into 2 outside threads.
L ch: Through 2.

Row 5 1 P, 1 tc dc, * 2 P, 1 tc dc, rep from * to last 2 st, 1 P, 1 tc dc into 2 outside threads.
L ch: Through 2.

Rows 6 to 9 As rows 2 to 5.
Rows 10 to 13 As rows 2 to 5.

Colour illustration opp. p. 71.

COMBINATION PATTERN

With 4 different tricot stitches.
P — purl, K — knit stitch, cr st — cross stitch, tc dc — plain or tricot double crochet stitch.
Worked over an even number of ch.

Make 28 ch.
Row 1 1 P into 2nd ch, 1 P into each ch to end.
L ch: Through 2.

Row 2 1 P into each f b to end.
L ch: Through 2.

Row 3 1 tc dc into next f b, 1 P into each of next 2 f b, 1 K into each of next 2 f b, 1 P into each of next 2 f b, 1 tc dc into each of next 2 f b, 1 P into each of next 2 f b, 1 cr st into next 2 f b, 1 cr st into 2 following f b, 1 P into each of next 2 f b, 1 tc dc into each of next 2 f b, 1 P into each of next 2 f b, 1 K into each of next 2 f b, 1 P into each of next 2 f b, 1 tc dc into next f b, 1 tc dc into 2 outside threads.
L ch: Through 2.
Rows 4 to 12 As row 3.

Finishing:
Work a row of slip stitches into front bars of last row for a neat finish to the piece.

79

WORKING WITH TRICOT

BASQUE AND BUTTON-BAND
This sample piece will illustrate the working of a perfect edge for a cardigan at the same time as making the bodice.

Make 20 ch.
Rows 1 to 5 P stitch foundation rows (basque). L ch: Through 2.
Row 6 Bodice and button-band or buttonhole-band: 8 P, tc dc to end. L ch: Through 2.
Rows 7 to 14 As row 6.

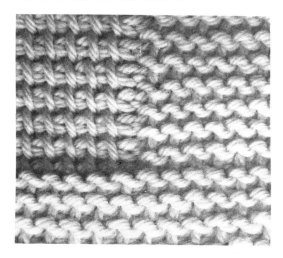

TRICOT PLAIN STITCH BUTTONHOLE
Make 11 ch.
Rows 1 to 3 Tc dc foundation rows. L ch: Through 2.
Row 4 Starting with rem lp on hook work 1 tc dc into each of next 3

f b, miss 3 f b (more for larger buttons), wind yarn around hook from back to front 3 times (as many times as the no of f b missed), 1 tc dc into next f b, tc dc to end. L ch: Through 2 counting each winding around hook as 1 loop.
Row 5 Tc dc row working st above buttonhole inserting hook into loops as shown by arrows on the illustration. L ch: Through 2.
Rows 6 to 10 Tc dc rows. L ch: Through 2.

PURL STITCH BUTTONHOLE
Make 16 ch.
Rows 1 to 5 P stitch rows. L ch: Through 2.
Row 6 6 P, miss 3 f b (or as many as required for button size), wind yarn around hook 3 times from the front to the back (as many times as the number of stitches missed), 1 P into next f b, P to end.
L ch: Through 2 counting each winding around hook as 1 loop.
Row 7 P row working stitches above buttonhole into the loops as in the tc dc buttonhole exercise. L ch: Through 2.

Rows 8 to 12 P stitch rows.
L ch: Through 2.

PATCHWORK

In tricot and Lace Tricot there is no need to work single patches and sew them together, it will never be a neat join. Work the patches in fair isle style taking the yarns evenly along the back of the work.

A simple chequer pattern in tc dc is given below as an example. You will notice on the illustration the A-line decrease in the pattern.

This was achieved by changing over to narrower hooks as the piece was worked, while the number of stitches in every row remained unchanged. (This technique of A-line increasing and decreasing is explained in Part I.)

The piece is worked in two contrasting colours, A and B.

Make 48 ch in A.
Row 1 (A) 1st tc dc into 2nd ch, 1 tc dc into each ch to end.
L ch: Through 2.
Row 2 1 tc dc into each of next 7 f b (A), * 1 tc dc into each of next 8 f b (B), 1 tc dc into each of next 8 f b (A), rep from * ending

with 8 tc dc in B.
L ch: Through 2, locking A stitches with A yarn and B stitches with B.
Rows 3 to 5 As row 2.
Rows 6 to 9 7 tc dc in B, (8 tc dc in A, 8 tc dc in B) to end.
L ch: Through 2, locking the stitches with yarn of corresponding colour.
Rows 10 to 13 As row 2.
Rows 14 to 17 As row 6.

POTHOLDER WITH AN APPLE

Materials
No. 2 crocheting cotton, 1 ball each red, green and foundation colour (white or beige)
Hook 4.50 (tricot) (no. 7) and crochet hook 4.50 (no. 7).

Make 32 ch (foundation colour).
Rows 1 to 3 Tc dc rows in foundation colour (L ch: Through 2).
Rows 4 to 24 Tc dc rows with L ch through 2 following the chart for colours and locking the stitches with their own colour in the lock chain. In the forward row simply pick up the new coloured yarn with the hook for the next stitch but in the lock chain make a twist with the yarns as you join in the new colours.

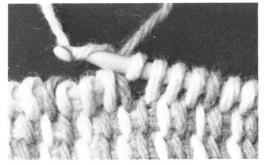

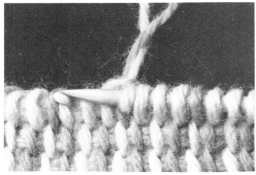

into corner stitches. Finish upper corner with 12 ch for a loop, sl st to 1st dc of round.

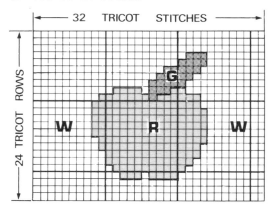

AFGHAN RUG
A beautiful decorative tricot rug with crochet edges.

Materials
800 g (28 oz) base colour
(e.g. dark green),
150 g (5 oz) yellow
75 g (3 oz) gold
125 g (4 oz) red
25 g (1 oz) each bone and rust
brown — all 12 ply wool
Hook 7.00 (tricot) (no. 2) and
crochet hook 7.00 (no. 2).

Using tricot hook make 128 ch in base colour.

Row 1 1st tc dc into 2nd ch from hook, 1 tc dc into each ch to end leaving all rem lp on hook and following the chart for colour pattern (128 tc dc in row).

Use separate balls for every colour patch in row. A good way of preventing the wool from getting entangled is to place the balls in a

Finishing
With the crochet hook (in green colour) work a round of dc into the edge, starting at the top right hand corner and working 3 dc

82

fruit carton, preferably with cardboard partitions for every ball and taking the strands of yarn through holes on the top or on the side.

L ch: Through 2 locking the stitches with their own colour — make a twist with the two colours at the joins as illustrated in the prev pattern.

Rows 2 to 99 Tc dc rows with L ch through 2 and colours worked from the chart.

Edges

With 7.00 crochet hook in base colour starting at one of the corners work 1 dc into 1st st. Work 2 rounds of dc right around the edges with 2 dc into each corner st and 1 dc into every other st. Sl st to 1st dc at the end of Round 2.

Round 3 5 ch, 1 ttr into same sp as 5 ch, 1 ch, 1 ttr into next dc, 2 ch

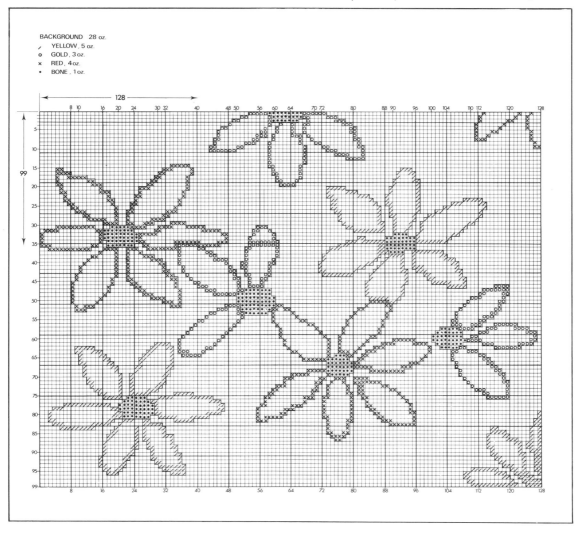

BACKGROUND 28 oz.
/ YELLOW, 5 oz.
o GOLD, 3 oz.
x RED, 4 oz.
• BONE, 1 oz.

miss 2 dc, 1 puff st, worked as follows: * yoh, insert hook into dc, yoh, draw through dc, pull up to 5 cm (2 in) *, rep from * to * 3 more times into same dc leaving all lp on hook (9 lp on hook), yoh, draw through 8 lp, yoh, draw through 2 lp (puff st completed), ** 2 ch, miss 2 dc, 1 puff st into next dc, rep from ** to last 3 dc in next corner, 2 ch, miss 1 dc, 1 ttr into next dc, 1 ch, 1 ttr into next dc, 1 ch, 1 ttr into same dc, 1 ch, 1 ttr into next dc, 2 ch, miss 1 dc, 1 puff st into next dc, *** 2 ch, miss 2 dc, 1 puff st into next dc, rep from *** to last 3 dc before

next corner, cont working the corners and edges thus to end, sl st to comm ch of round.

Rounds 4 and 5 Work these two rounds in dc around the outside edge to give your rug a perfectly neat finish.

Colour illustration opp. p. 86.

TRICOT EDGING

Excellent edges can be worked in tricot and in Lace Tricot. Around the neck and armholes of a garment a round of double crochet (dc and *not* tc dc) worked with the crochet hook will serve as the foundation for an edge such as the one illustrated in this exercise.

In the practice piece we shall work the edging pattern into a ch instead of dc.

Make 30 ch.

Tricot edge row: Yoh, insert hook into 2nd ch, yoh, draw it through ch leaving loops on hook, *yoh, insert hook into next ch, yoh, draw it through ch leaving rem loops on hook, rep from * to end into each ch.

L ch: Once through 2, then through 3 to last rem 2 lp, once through 2, once through 1 for fastening off.

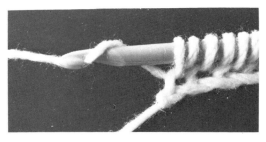

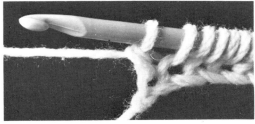

GARMENTS IN TRICOT

CARDIGAN FOR BOY OR GIRL

Materials
For girl 16 (18, 20) balls 8 ply wool
For boy 17 (19, 21) balls 8 ply wool
Tricot hook 4.50 (no. 7), pr of
knitting needles no. 10, 5 buttons.

Measurements
To fit 66 (71, 76) cm chest
(26, 28, 30 in)
Length from shoulder:
girl: 39 (42, 46) cm
         (15½, 16½, 18 in)
boy: 42 (45, 48) cm
         (16½, 17½, 19 in)
Length of sleeve: 32 (36, 39) cm
(12½, 14, 15½ in) or as required.
Tension: 20 tc dc to 10 cm (4 in).

BACK
Using tricot hook make 74 (78, 84) ch.
Foundation row Insert hook into 2nd
ch from hook, yoh, draw a lp through
leaving it on hook, draw a lp through
each ch to end leaving all lp on hook.
74 (78, 84) lp.
L ch: Draw a lp through 1st lp on
hook, * draw a lp through 2 lp, rep
from * to end, 1 lp rem on hook to
start next row.
Row 2 Lp on hook stands for 1st st,
draw a lp through next f b leaving it on
hook, draw a lp through each f b to
end, 74 (78, 84) sts.
L ch: As foundation row, this is to be
repeated throughout.
Rep row 2 until work measures for
girl 21.5 (23, 25.5) cm (8½, 9, 10 in),
for boy 24 (26.5, 28) cm (9½, 10½,
11 in) or length required.

Shape Raglan Next row: (Draw a lp

through next f b and lp on hook)
twice, work to the last 2 f b, * (2 st
decr each end).

1st decr row: Draw a lp through next
f b (2 lp on hook), insert hook through
next 2 f b, draw 1 lp through, draw
1 lp through each f b to last 4 f b,
insert hook through next 2 f b, draw
1 lp through, draw 1 lp through each
of next 2 f b, * (thus 1 st decr each
end of row).
Next row Work without decr.
Rep last 2 rows 4 times, then work
1st decr row every row until there are
20 (20, 22) lp on hook.
Sl st across rem stitches thus (draw
a lp through next f b and lp on
hook) to end, fasten off.

BASQUE
Right side facing using no. 10
knitting needles pick up and knit 78
(84, 88) sts along lower edge.   Work
in K1, P1 rib for 4 cm (1½ in).
Cast off in rib.

LEFT FRONT
Make 36 (38, 41) ch.
Foundation row As for back.   36
(38, 41) loops.
Cont as back until work measures
same as Back to Armhole.

Shape Raglan Armhole and Front
Next row Sl st across 2 f b, patt to
last 2 f b, draw 1 lp through next
2 f b leaving 33 (35, 38) lp.
Row 1 Draw a lp through next f b
(2 lp on hook), insert hook through
next 2 f b, draw 1 lp through, work
patt to end, 32 (34, 37) loops.
Row 2 Work without decr.
Row 3 Draw a lp through next f b

85

(2 lp on hook), work next 2 f b together, patt to last 2 f b, work last 2 together, 30 (32, 35) loops.

Row 4 Work without decr.

Row 5 As row 1, 29 (31, 34) sts.

Row 6 Draw a lp through each f b to last 2, work last 2 together.

Row 7 As row 1, 27 (29, 32) loops.

Row 8 Work without decr.

Row 9 As row 3, 25 (27, 30) loops.

Row 10 Work without decr.

Row 11 As row 1, 24 (26, 29) loops.

Row 12 As row 3, 22 (24, 27) loops.

Row 13 As row 1, 21 (23, 26) loops.

Row 14 As row 1, 20 (22, 25) loops.

Row 15 As row 3, 18 (20, 23) loops.

Rep rows 13 to 15 2 (2, 3) times.

Cont to work 3rd and 4th sts tog every row until 4 loops remain in last row.

Next row Work 2 last f b together (3 loops).

Rep last row Once (2 loops), I ch to lock off, 1 lp left on hook. Draw a lp through this lp and fasten off.

BASQUE

With right side facing using no. 10 knitting needles pick up and knit 40 (42, 36) sts along lower edge. Work in K1, P1 rib for 4 cm (1½ in). Cast off in rib.

RIGHT FRONT

Work as Left Front to underarm.

Shape Raglan Armhole and Front

Draw a lp through next f b and lp on hook (1 st decr), work to last 2 f b 33 (35, 38) loops. lock off by I ch.

Row 1 Work to last 4 f b, work 2

86

tog, then work into each of next 2, 32 (34, 37).

Row 2 Work without decr.

Row 3 Draw a lp through next f b and lp on hook, work patt to last 4 f b, work 2 tog, last 2 st without decr, 30 (32, 35).

Row 4 As row 2.

Row 5 As row 1, 29 (31, 34) sts.

Row 6 Draw a lp through next f b and lp on hook, work patt to end.

Row 7 As row 1, 27 (29, 32) loops.

Row 8 As row 2.

Row 9 As row 3, 25 (27, 30) sts.

Row 10 As row 2.

Row 11 As row 1, 24 (26, 29) loops.

Row 12 As row 3, 22 (24, 27) loops.

Row 13 As row 1, 21 (23, 26) loops.

Row 14 As row 1, 20 (22, 25) loops.

Row 15 As row 3, 18 (20, 23) loops.

Rep rows 13 to 15 2 (2, 3) times.

Cont in patt working 3rd and 4th last f b together every row until 4 loops only remain in last row.

Next row Work first 2 f b together (3 loops).

Rep last row (2 loops), work I ch and fasten off.

BASQUE

As for left front.

Place 5 markers on front edge equal distances apart, left side for girl or right side for boy, having the top one at first neck decr and lowest one 2 cm (¾ in) from lower edge.

SLEEVES

Make 38 (40, 42) ch.

Foundation row As for back, 38 (40, 42) loops.

Cont in pattern for 5 more rows.

Incr row 1 ch, draw a lp through f b

at edge of row, then through each
f b to last, yoh, draw a lp through
rem f b, 40 (42, 44) loops or 1 st
incr at each end.
Next 3 rows Work without incr.
Rep last 4 rows 3 times.
Cont in patt incr 1 st at each end of
every 4th following row to 58 (62,
66) sts.
Cont in patt until sleeve measures
27 (31, 34) cm (10½, 12, 13½ in)
or 5 cm (2 in) less than length
required.

Raglan Shaping
Work as Back shaping until 6 st
remain in row.
Next row Cont in patt without decr.
Last row Sl st across all sts and
fasten off.

CUFF
With right side facing using no. 10
knitting needles pick up and knit
38 (40, 42) sts along the lower edge.
Work in K1, P1 rib for 5 cm (2 in).
Cast off in rib.

FRONT BAND
With no. 10 knitting needles cast on
11 sts.
Row 1 (K1, P1) to last st, K1.
Row 2 (P1, K1) to last st, P1.
Rows 3 to 6 As rows 1 and 2.
Buttonhole row
Rib 4, cast off 3, rib 4.
Next row Rib 4, cast on 3, rib 4.
Cont rib making 4 more buttonholes
opposite markers stretching band
slightly.
Cont in rib until band is long enough
when slightly stretched to reach up
one front, around back of neck and

down the other side front to lower
edge.
Cast off in rib.

To make up
Press on wrong side being careful not
to stretch the edges. Join the four
raglan seams, side seams and sleeves.
Join band to fronts stretching band
and easing edges so that left and
right sides are the same length,
buttonholes on right front for girl or
left front for boy.

JACKET FOR GIRL

Materials
10 (12, 14) balls 8 ply wool, white
Small quantity of wool in two pastel
shades

87

Ladies' mohair coat (p. 110).

Hook 4.50 (no. 7) (tricot) and crochet hook 3.50 (no. 9), 2 buttons.

Measurements

To fit 51 (61, 66) cm chest (22, 24, 26 in).
Length from shoulder: 30.5 (34.5, 39.5) cm (12, 13½, 15½ in).
Length of sleeve seam: 23 (28, 33) cm (9, 11, 13 in).
Tension: 20 tc dc to 10 cm.(4 inch)

BACK

With tricot hook make 64 (69, 74) ch.

Row 1 Miss 1 ch, * draw a lp through next ch leaving it on hook, rep from * to end, 64 (69, 74) loops.
L ch: yoh, draw through 1st st, * yoh, draw through 2 lp, rep from * to end, 1 lp left on hook to stand for 1st st of next row.
Row 2 Insert hook into next f b, draw 1 lp through leaving it on hook, cont working tc dc to last f b, last tc dc into 2 outer threads, 64 (69, 74) sts.
Rep row 2 until work measures 19 (21.5, 25.5) cm (7½, 8½, 10 in) or 1.5 cm (½ in) less than required length for underarm.

Shape armholes

* Draw a lp through next f b and lp on hook (1 st decr), rep from * twice more, tc dc to last 3 f b, don't work into last 3 f b, 58 (63, 68) lp on hook.
Decr row Decr 1 st each end: draw a lp through next f b and lp on hook, tc dc into each f b to last 2 f b, insert hook into last 2 f b,

draw 1 lp through, 56 (61, 66) lp.
Next 3 rows Rep last row, 50 (55, 60) sts.
Cont even until armholes measure 10 (11.5, 13) cm (4, 4½, 5 in) on the straight.

Shape shoulder

Sl st across 1st 7 (8, 9) sts, tc dc into each f b to last 7 (8, 9) sts.
Next row Sl st across next 7 (8, 9) sts, tc dc to last 7 (8, 9) f b.
Next row Sl st across 22 (23, 24) back neck sts, sl st across 14 (16, 18) sts of left shoulder, fasten off.

LEFT FRONT

Make 30 (33, 35) ch.
Row 1 As row 1 of back, 30 (33, 35) lp on hook.
Cont working in patt until work measures same as back to underarm.

Shape armhole

Sl st across 1st 3 sts, patt to end.
Next 4 rows Decr 1 st at beg of each row, 23 (26, 28) sts.
Cont even until armhole measures 6 (6.5, 7) cm (2¼, 2½, 2¾ in) on the straight.

Shape neck

Next row Tc dc into each f b to last 4 sts. Cont patt, 1 decr st at neck edge on next 5 (6, 6) rows, 14 (16, 18) sts.
Cont on rem sts until armhole matches back armhole.

Shape shoulder

Sl st across 1st 7 (8, 9) sts, tc dc to end.
Next row Sl st across rem 7 (8, 9) sts.

RIGHT FRONT

Work as left front to underarm.
Next row Tc dc to last 3 sts.
Next 4 rows Tc dc rows with 1 decr st at armhole edge, (23, 26, 28) sts. Cont even until armhole measures 6 (6.5, 7) cm (2¼, 2½, 2¾ in) on the straight.

Shape neck

Next row Sl st across 1st 4 sts, tc dc to end.
Following rows 5 (6, 6) rows tc dc with 1 decr st at neck edge in every row, 14 (16, 18) sts. Cont on rem sts until armhole measures same as back armhole.

Shape shoulder

Next row 1 tc dc into each of next 7 (8, 9) f b.
Last row Sl st across all 14 (16, 18) sts (prev 2 rows).
Fasten off.

SLEEVES

Make 32 (35, 37) ch.
Rows 1 to 6 Tc dc rows, 32 (35, 37) loops.

Incr row 1 ch, draw a lp through 1st f b at edge of row, (1 tc dc incr) 1 tc dc into each f b to end, 1 tc dc into each of the 2 outer threads (another 1 tc dc incr).
Cont in patt, incr 1 tc dc each end of every 6th foll row to 42 (47, 53) sts.
Cont in patt until sleeve measures

21.5 (26.5, 31.5) cm (8½, 10½, 12½ in) or 1.5 cm (½ in) less than length required.

Shape top

Sl st across 1st 3 sts, tc dc to last 3 sts.
Cont in patt decr 1 st each end of every row until 16 (17, 19) sts rem.
Next row Sl st across all sts and fasten off.

To make up

Press on wrong side with warm iron over damp cloth. Seam shoulders and sides. Seam sleeves and set into armholes.

EDGING

Using the crochet hook and a pastel shade work a round of dc around all edges, 2 dc into corner sts and being careful not to stretch the edges.
With white, work another round of dc into foundation (pastel) round working 2 dc again into corner sts and 1 decr dc at each shoulder seam. With second pastel shade work the last dc edging round into the white round. Fasten off.
Work rounds of dc around each cuff in the same manner.
Press all seams and edgings.

Sew a button at each side of the neck edge. Work a crochet chain loop and join in the middle and slip over each button.

TRICOT TREBLE STITCHES

TRICOT "TREBLE" STITCHES

Here I will illustrate to you two already existing types of stitches which have been termed tricot or Tunisian crochet trebles. I prefer the term half treble (tc htr) for reasons outlined below.

Textures produced by working these stitches — as you will realise — will slant; the edges will not develop in right angle to the foundation row, however carefully and uniformly you try to work them. They are practically useless in themselves for producing a well-formed garment but are sometimes built into Afghan stitch patterns, the plain stitch correcting their balance, as in the case of a top shoulder row with a decrease slant.

Half Treble 1

Make 30 ch.

Row 1 Yoh, insert hook into 3rd ch from hook, yoh, draw it through ch, yoh, draw it through next 2 lp leaving rem lp on hook, *yoh, insert hook into next ch, yoh, draw it through ch, yoh, draw it through 2 lp leaving rem lp on hook *, work tc htr into each ch to end as from * to *.
L ch: Once through 1, through 2 to end.

Row 2 2 ch, 1 tc htr into each f b to end working tc htr as in row 1 but into f b instead of ch.
L ch: Once through 1, through 2

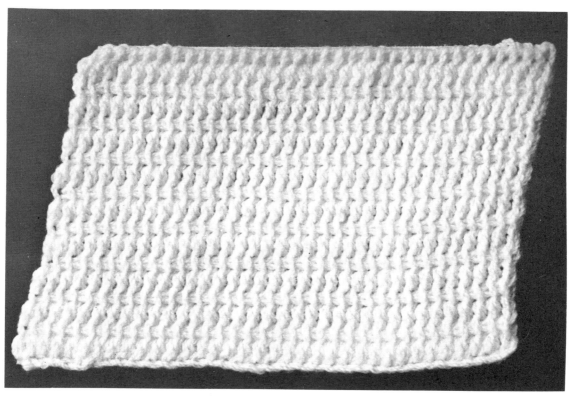

to end.
Rows 3 to 10 As row 2.

The sample illustrated was worked very tightly to show that the slanting is not due to loose stitching.

Half treble 2
Make 32 ch.
Row 1 1 half treble into 4th ch from hook as follows: * yoh, insert hook into ch, yoh, draw it through ch, yoh, draw through 1 lp on hook, yoh, draw through next 2 lp on hook leaving rem lp on hook *, 1 tr htr into each ch as from * to * to end.
L ch: Once through 1, through 2 to end.
Row 2 2 ch, 1 tr htr into each f b to end worked as in row 1 * to * but inserting hook into f b.
L ch: As for row 1.
Rows 3 to 10 As row 2.

PART III

Lace Tricot

INTRODUCTION

In Parts I and II of this book two age-old arts have been described: crochet and tricot crochet.

Lace Tricot is something new, something as modern as the age in which we live. Lace Tricot provides an answer to knitters and crocheters who have always yearned to make garments and articles with beautiful textures; articles which do not stretch, drop, sag or bag; articles which can be made quickly.

The tools of Lace Tricot are the knitting yarn and the tricot hook; these are familiar to us from the previous pages of this book and from experience. But we now learn a new trick: to make balanced trebles by building in a balancing stitch on top of every treble. The results are: no slanting of the fabric, and the possibility of working a large variety of lace-like or crochet-like or just simply Lace Tricot-like patterns.

And it is fast, too: there are many less rows of treble, double treble or triple treble to a given length than in a crocheted article and firmness is improved.

I hope you enjoy working in Lace Tricot.

For general instructions on designing, edging, and so on, see also Part II (Tricot).

Note: Patent has been applied for Lace Tricot in a number of countries ("New method of stitching"). Individuals should feel free to use Lace Tricot for non-commercial purposes. Publication of patterns and the sale of Lace Tricot garments in commercial quantities are subject to licensing arrangements.

ON WORKING LACE TRICOT

The basic stitches in Lace Tricot are *trebles:* treble, double treble and triple treble.

As in tricot, after completing these stitches the remaining loop always stays on the hook. Remember this basic rule, as it will not be mentioned in the description of the practice samples. At the end of the row the loops are worked off by the lock chain.

Holding the tricot hook
Hold the hook as you hold the crochet hook. Some people may find it easier to work tricot and Lace Tricot holding the hook in the fist.

TREBLE STITCH
This stitch is the basis of all Lace Tricot work. Make sure you do not confuse it with tricot treble or Tunisian treble stitches which were described in Part II as half trebles.

We will adopt the abbreviation T for Lace Tricot treble stitch or stitches.

Make 22 ch.
Row 1 Miss 3 ch, * yoh, insert hook into next ch,

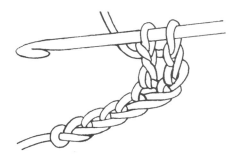

yoh, draw it through ch,

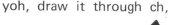

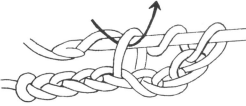

yoh, draw it through 2 lp on hook,

yoh, draw through 1 lp leaving rem

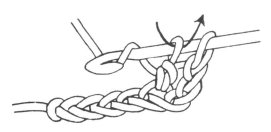

lp on hook * (1 T completed).

The important last looping gives the balance to the texture, preventing it from slanting from left to right. Never forget this step as it has to be included in every stitch to make it a genuine workable treble.

Rep from * to * into next ch and into each ch to end, leaving all rem lp on hook.

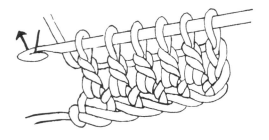

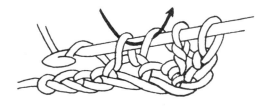

Locking off the stitches of the row is called the *lock chain* and it is worked similarly to the lock chain of tricot rows.

L ch: Through 2 to end, worked as follows:

yoh, draw through next 2 lp on hook, * yoh, draw through next 2 lp on hook (counting lp on hook as

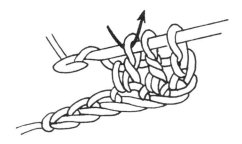

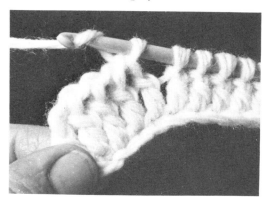

1st lp and upper lp of next st as 2nd lp), rep from * to end, untie and you have 1 lp left on hook.

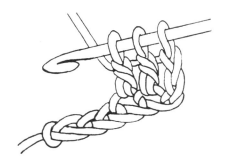

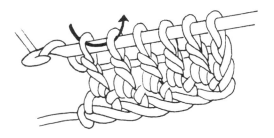

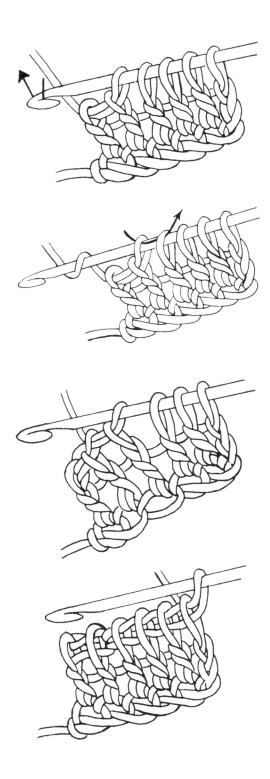

The work in Lace Tricot is *not* turned.

Row 2 2 ch (to stand for 1st T in row).

You observe now that the front half of the upper loops in the first row show clearly. These front halves are called the *front bars* (f b) as in tricot — they are the part of the stitch into which we work the stitches of the next row.

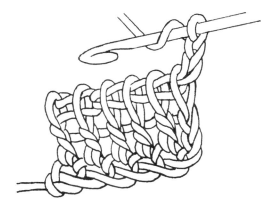

Never work into the front bar directly under the beginning chains.

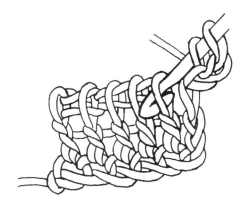

* yoh, insert hook into next f b, draw 1 lp through, yoh, draw through next 2 lp, yoh, draw through 1 lp leaving rem lp on hook *,

rep from * to * into each f b to end leaving rem loops on hook.
L ch: Through 2 to end.

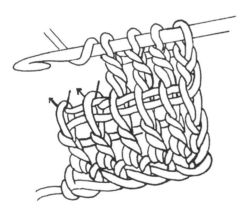

The trebles are exactly one above the other; at the end of the row make sure that you work into both the 2nd last and into the last front bar even though these two last stitches are looped together with the lock chain.

Rows 3 to 5 As row 2.

Fastening off:

After completing last lock chain in the last row, break yarn off about 10 cm (4 in) from last loop, draw this remaining yarn through the last loop, tighten. Sew the loose piece of yarn neatly into the back of work with a wool needle.

DOUBLE TREBLE
(abbreviated DT)

Make 20 ch.
Row 1 Miss 4 ch, * yoh twice, insert hook into next ch,

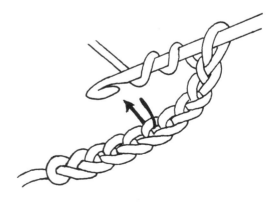

yoh, draw it through ch,

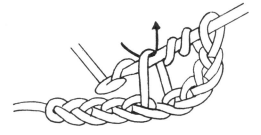

yoh, draw through next 2 lp on hook,

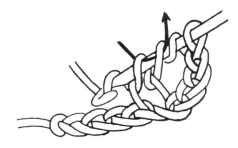

yoh, draw through following 2 lp,

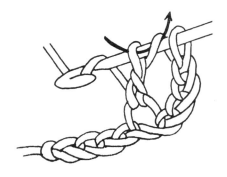

yoh, draw through 1 lp on hook leaving rem lp on hook * (DT completed), work DT into each ch to end as from * to * leaving all rem lp on hook.

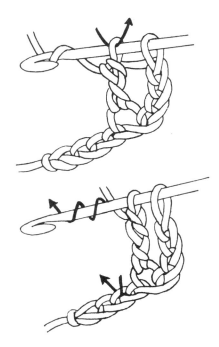

L ch: Through 2 to end.
Row 2 3 ch, * yoh twice, insert hook into next f b, yoh, draw through, yoh, draw through 2, yoh, draw through 2 again, yoh, draw through 1 leaving rem lp on hook * Work DT into each f b to end as from * to * leaving all rem lp on hook.
L ch: Through 2.
Row 3 and following rows As row 2.

TRIPLE TREBLE OR
LONG TREBLE
(abbreviated LT)

Make 30 ch.

Row 1 yoh, three times, insert hook into 6th ch, yoh, draw 1 lp through ch, (yoh, draw through 2 lp on hook) 3 times, yoh, draw through 1 lp leaving rem lp on hook (first LT completed), * yoh 3 times, insert hook into next ch, yoh, draw 1 lp through ch, (yoh, draw through 2) 3 times, yoh, draw through 1 leaving rem lp on hook, rep from * to end leaving all rem lp on hook.
L ch: Through 2 to end.

Row 2 4 ch, * yoh 3 times, insert hook into next f b, yoh, draw through f b, (yoh, draw through 2) 3 times, yoh, draw through 1 lp leaving rem lp on hook, rep from * to end leaving all rem lp on hook.
L ch: Through 2.

Row 3 and following rows As row 2.

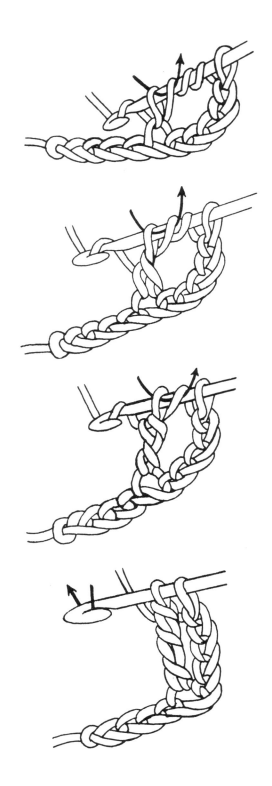

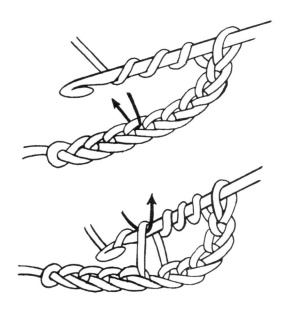

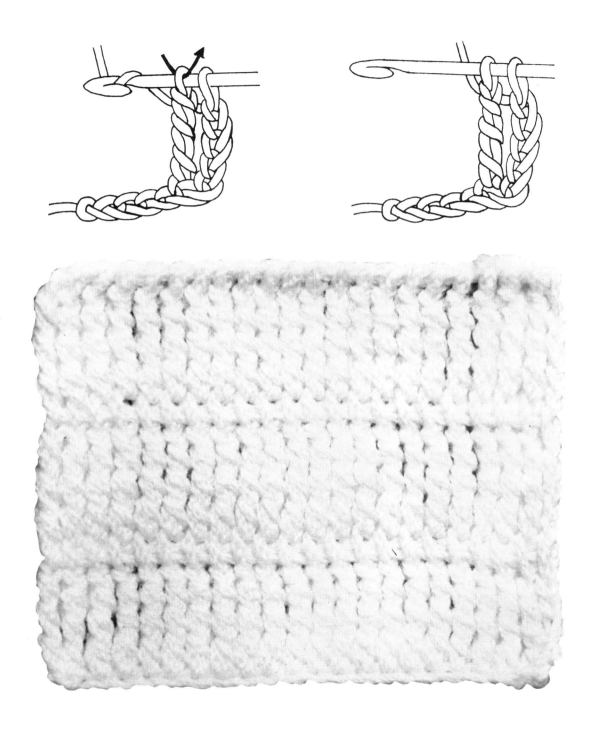

DECREASING AND INCREASING

There are two ways of decreasing illustrated in the following treble decrease/increase exercises. The same techniques can — of course — be applied to double and triple trebles.

1. Treble decreasing and increasing
Make 30 ch.
Row 1 1st T into 4th ch, 1 T into each ch to end.
L ch: Through 2.
Row 2 2 ch, insert hook into next 2 f b and work 1 T into the 2 f b (1 T decr), 1 T into each f b to rem 3 f b, 1 T into next 2 f b (another T decr), 1 T into last f b.
L ch: Through 2.
Rows 3 to 13 T rows with decr in every 2nd and 3rd and every 3rd last and 2nd last f b in each row (4 T remain).

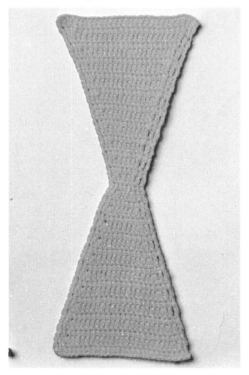

Row 14 incr row: 2 ch, 2 T into next f b, 1 T into each f b to rem 2 f b, 2 T into following f b, 1 T into last f b.
L ch: Through 2.
Rows 15 to 26 T rows with incr: work 2 T into 2nd and 2 T into 2nd last f b in each row.
L ch: Through 2.

2. Another treble decrease
Make 24 ch.
Row 1 1st T into 4th ch from hook, 1 T into each ch to end.
L ch: Through 2.
Row 2 2 ch, 1 T into next f b, * yoh, insert hook into next f b, yoh, draw through f b, yoh, draw through 2 lp leaving lp on hook, yoh, insert hook into next f b, yoh, draw through f b, yoh, draw through 2 lp, yoh, draw through the 2 upper loops of the half trebles

just worked * (1 T decreased very neatly). Work 1 T into each f b to last 4 f b, 1 T decr as from * to *,

104

1 T into each of last 2 f b.

L ch: Through 2.

Cont decr every 3rd and 4th and every 4th and 3rd last T in each row until there are 6 T left in row.

3. Armhole decrease

Make 26 ch.

Row 1 1 T into 4th ch, 1 T into each ch to end.

L ch: Through 2.

Row 2 2 ch, 1 T into each f b to end.

L ch: Through 2.

Row 3 Sl st into each of next 8 f b, 2 ch, 1 decr T as follows: * yoh, insert hook into next f b, yoh, draw through f b, yoh, draw through 2 lp, yoh, insert hook into next f b, yoh, draw through f b, yoh, draw through 2 lp, yoh, draw through the 2 upper loops of half trebles * (1 T

decreased), 1 T into each f b to end.

L ch: Through 2.

Row 4 2 ch, 1 decr T as from * to * in prev row, 1 T into each f b to end.

L ch: Through 2.

Row 5 As row 4.

4. Dart decreasing and increasing

Make 32 ch.

Row 1 1 T into 4th ch, 1 T into each ch to end.

L ch: Through 2.

Row 2 2 ch, 1 T into each of next 7 f b, yoh, insert hook into next 2 f b for 1 T (1 T decr), 1 T into each of next 10 f b, yoh, insert hook into 2 f b for next T (another T decr), 1 T into each of rem 8 f b.

L ch: Through 2.

Rows 3 to 6 2 ch, 7 T, 1 decr T, 1 T into each f b to 10th last f b, 1 decr T (10th and 9th last st worked together), 8 T.

L ch: As for prev rows.

The number of stitches on both sides of the darts should be kept equal.

Row 7 and following rows (incr):
T rows working 2 T into every 9th
f b and 2 T into every 9th last
f b in each row until you have
again the starting width of 30 T.
You will notice that the dart
decrease shows very clearly while the
increase is hardly visible.

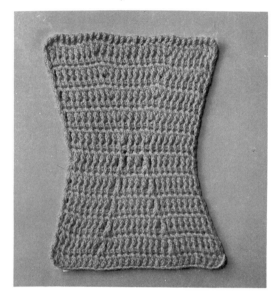

SKIRT

Materials
300 (350, 400) g (11, 13, 15 oz)
12 ply crepe wool in bright colour
Hook 4.50 (no. 7) and zip fastener.

Measurements
To fit 61 (66, 71) cm (24, 26, 28
in) waist and 86 (91, 96) cm
(34, 36, 38 in) hip.
To adjust length, work additional
rows up to decr darts.

Tension: 9 treble to 5 cm (2 in),
8 rows to 13 cm (5 in).

FRONT
Make a firm ch of 83 (88, 92).
Row 1 1 T into 4th ch, 1 T into
each ch to end.
L ch: Through 2 to end.
Row 2 2 ch, 1 T into next f b,
1 T into each f b to end.
L ch: As for row 1.
Rows 3 to 15 As row 2.
Row 16 Dart decr row: T row
working 15th and 16th f b together
for 1 T and 16th last with 15th last
f b for 1 T.
L ch: Through 2.
Rows 17 to 26 As row 16.
L ch of row 26 casts off the front
half.

BACK
Work same as the front.

Finishing off
Join rows and seams firmly, sew
with flat seam leaving 12 cm (5 in)
open for zip fastener on the left side.
Sew in zip fastener.

BELT
No elastic band is needed.
Make a ch of 160 with double yarn,
sew in the ends of loose yarn and
make tight knots at the ends. Pull
this belt through the upper row of
the skirt alternating 2 T in front and
2 T behind. Knot above the zip
fastener on left side.

LACE TRICOT PATTERNS

TWO-TONE PATTERN

In treble and tricot plain stitches. Worked over a multiple of 5 plus 6 ch in colours *A* and *B*.

Make 26 ch in *A*.
Row 1 1 T into 4th ch from hook, 1 T into each ch to end.
L ch: Through 2.
Row 2 Join in *B*, yoh, draw through lp on hook, 1 tc dc into each of next 3 f b (working of tc dc: insert hook into f b, draw 1 lp through, leaving lp on hook), * 1 T around body of next T, 1 tc dc into each of next 4 f b, rep from * to end.
L ch: Through 2 to end, then change to *A*.
Row 3 2 ch, 1 T into each f b to end.
L ch: Through 2.
Row 4 (in *B*) As row 2.
Row 5 (in *A*) As row 3.

Such a pattern could be used in cardigans and many other garments.

SPIDER PATTERN

(Crossed stitches)
Worked over an even no. of ch.

Make 24 ch.

Row 1 1 T into 4th ch from hook, 1 T into each ch to end.
L ch: Through 2.
Row 2 2 ch, * miss 1 f b, 1 T into next f b, 1 T into missed f b, rep from * to last f b, 1 T into last f b.
L ch: Through 2.
Rows 3 to 7 As row 2.
Row 8 2 ch, 1 T into each f b to end.
L ch: Through 2.

CROSS STITCH — DECREASING

Such decreasing is useful when working skirt or coat patterns.

Make 68 ch.
Row 1 1 T into 4th ch, 1 T into each ch to end.
L ch: Through 2.
Row 2 2 ch, work 1 crossed treble as follows: miss next f b, 1 T into following f b, 1 T into missed f b (cr T completed), cont working cr T to last f b, 1 T into last f b.
L ch: Through 2.
Row 3 1st decr row: 2 ch, 9 cr T, draw through 2 f b for next 1 T, 12 cr T, 1 T into next 2 f b (2nd decr), 9 cr T, 1 T into last f b.

L ch: Through 2.

Row 4 2 ch, 9 cr T, miss 2 f b, 1 T into next f b, draw through the 2 missed f b for next T, 10 cr T, miss 2 f b, 1 T into next f b, draw through 2 missed f b for next T, 9 cr T, 1 T into last f b.

L ch: Through 2.

Rows 5 to 6 2 ch, crossed T to last f b, 1 T into last f b.

L ch: Through 2.

Row 7 2 ch, 9 cr T, 1 T into next 2 f b, 10 cr T, 1 T into next f b, 9 cr T, 1 T into last f b.

L ch: Through 2.

Row 8 2 ch, 9 cr T, miss 2 f b, 1 T into next f b, 1 T into the 2 missed f b, 8 cr T, miss 2 f b, 1 T into next f b, 1 T into the 2 missed f b, 9 cr T, 1 T into last f b.

L ch: Through 2.

Rows 9 to 10 2 ch, cr T to last f b, 1 T into last f b.

L ch: Through 2.

Row 11 2 ch, 9 cr T, 1 T into next 2 f b, 8 cr T, 1 T into next 2 f b, 9 cr T, 1 T into last f b.

L ch: Through 2.

Row 12 2 ch, 9 cr T, miss 2 f b, 1 T into next f b, 1 T into 2 missed f b, 7 cr T, miss 2 f b, 1 T into next f b, 1 T into 2 missed f b, 9 cr T, 1 T into last f b.

L ch: Through 2.

Row 13 2 ch, cr T to last f b,

1 T into last f b.
L ch: Through 2.

Crossed trebles give a nice three-dimensional texture; they can be used in practically any garment, rug, cot cover etc. by themselves or in combination with other treble patterns.

TREBLE GROUP PATTERN
Worked over an uneven number of ch.

Make 21 ch.
Row 1 1 T into 4th ch, 1 T .into each ch to end.
L ch: (Through 1, through 3) to end.
Row 2 2 ch, 2 T into next ch space looping under small connecting bar between the T-groups, 2 T into each ch sp to last sp, 1 T into last sp, 1 T into f b of last T.
L ch: Through 2, (through 1,

through 3) to last rem T, once through 1, once through 2 loops.
Row 3 2 ch, 1 T into 1st sp (loop always under the connecting bar between the T-groups), 2 T into each ch sp to end, 1 T into f b of last T.
L ch: (Through 1-3) to end.
Row 4 As row 2.
Row 5 As row 3.

NET PATTERN
Worked over an uneven number of ch.

Make 25 ch.
Row 1 1st T into 5th ch from hook, * miss 1 ch, 1 T into next ch, rep from * to end.

L ch: (Through 1, through 2) to end.
Row 2 2 ch, miss next ch sp, 1 T into next f b, * miss next ch sp, 1 T into next f b, rep from * to end.
L ch: As row 1.
Rows 3 to 10 As row 2.

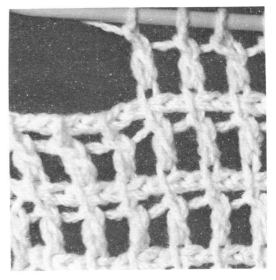

A fresh looking, loose but firm, non-stretch pattern for summer wear in fine yarn for men and women. Ideal for a sleeveless beach top — worked over a treble foundation row.

TREBLE CLUSTER PATTERN
Worked over a multiple of 7 plus 8 ch.

Make 36 ch.
Row 1 1 T into 4th ch, 1 T into each of next 3 ch, * miss 1 ch, 1 T into next ch, miss 1 ch, 1 T into each of next 4 ch, rep from * to last ch, 1 T into last ch.
L ch: * 4 times through 2, once through 1, once through 2, once through 1, rep from * to last 5 T, 5 times through 2.
Row 2 2 ch, * 1 T into each of next 4 f b, miss (1 ch, 1 T), 1 T into next 1-ch sp looping under connecting bar between T's, ** yoh, insert hook into missed 1-ch sp around T just worked and also under the connecting bar, yoh, draw through **, rep from ** to ** twice, yoh, draw through 6 lp, yoh, draw through 1 lp leaving upper lp of T and cluster gr on hook, rep from * to last 5 f b, 1 T into each

of last 5 f b.
L ch: *** 4 times through 2, once through 1, once through 3, once through 1, 4 times through 2, rep from *** to last once through 2.
Rows 3 to 12 As row 2.

LADIES' MOHAIR COAT
A fine mohair garment that does not stretch; warm, elegant and cosy. With or without lining.

Materials
800 g (28 oz) mohair
Hook 5.50 (no. 5)
Lining, if required; buttons.

Measurements
To fit bust: 86 cm (34 in)
To fit hip: 91 cm (36 in)
Sleeve length: 45 cm on seam
(17½ in)
Length: 81 cm (32 in); for additional length if required, add extra rows before decr for darts.
Tension: 8 T to 5 cm (2 in), 3 rows to 8 cm (3 in).

BACK
Make 99 ch.
Row 1 1 T into 4th ch from hook, 1 T into each ch to end.
L ch: Yoh, draw through 2 lp, rep through 2 to end.
Row 2 2 ch, 1 T into next f b, 1 cl into next f b as follows: yoh, draw 1 lp through f b leaving 1 lp on hook, yoh, draw through same f b (4 lp on hook), yoh, draw through same f b again (6 lp on hook), yoh, draw through 6 lp on hook, yoh, draw through rem 1 lp, leaving last rem lp on hook.

* 1 T into each of next 3 f b,
1 cl (cluster) into following f b, rep
from * to last 2 f b, 1 T into each
of next 2 f b.
L ch: Through 2.
Rows 3 to 12 As row 2.
Row 13 Work in patt to and incl
6th cl, decr 1 T (by working 1 T
into next 2 f b), 1 T into next f b,
1 cl into next f b, cont patt to and
incl 12th cl, 1 decr T, 1 T into next
f b, 1 cl into next f b, cont patt
to end.
L ch: As for prev rows.

Row 14 Work in patt, 2 T between
6th and 7th cl from each side.
Row 15 Cont patt with 1 T into
2 f b between 6th and 7th cl from
each side.
Row 16 In patt with 1 T between
6th and 7th cl each side.
Row 17 Cluster decrease: loop
through f b's of 6th cl-1 T-7th cl
for 1 cl decr each side.
Row 18 1 T decr between 6th and
7th cl each side.
Row 19 2 T between 6th and 7th
cl each side.
Row 20 1 decr T between 6th and
7th cl each side.
Row 21 1 T between 6th and 7th
cl each ·side.
Row 22 As row 17.
Rows 23 to 25 Work straight in patt.
Row 26 Armhole shaping: 1 sl st to
each of next 4 f b, 2 ch, cont patt
to last 5 f b, 1 tc dc into each of
next 5 f b (tc dc: insert hook into
f b, draw 1 lp through leaving rem
lp on hook).
L ch: Once through 1, 4 times
through 2, 2 ch, through 2 to end.
Rows 27 to 29 1 T decr each side

by looping through 2nd and 3rd f b
for 1 T and 3rd last and 2nd last
f b for 1 T.
Rows 30 to 35 Work straight in patt,
cast off with L ch through 2 to end
in last row.

RIGHT FRONT
Make 55 ch.
Row 1 T foundation row.
Rows 2 to 12 2 ch, 9 T for
buttonhole band, 1 cl into next f b,
work in patt to end as for the back.
Row 13 1 decr T between 6th and
7th cl from side edge left of work.
Row 14 2 T between last 6th and
7th cl.
Row 15 1 decr T between last 6th
and 7th cl.
Row 16 1 T between 6th and 7th cl.
Row 17 Dec 1 cl as back.
Row 18 1 decr T between last 6th
and 7th cl.
Row 19 2 T between last 6th and
7th cl.
Row 20 1 decr T between last 6th
and 7th cl.
Row 21 1 T between last 6th and
7th cl.
Row 22 1 cl dec into last (6th cl-
next T-7th cl).
Rows 23 to 25 Work straight in patt.
Row 26 Armhole shaping: Cont in
patt to last 7 f b, 1 tc dc into each
of last 7 f b.
L ch: Once through 1, 6 times
through 2, 2 ch, through 2 to end.
Rows 27 to 28 1 T decr left side
only.
Rows 29 to 32 Work straight in patt.

Shape neck
Row 33 12 sl st, 2 ch, patt to end.

111

Rows 34 to 35 1 T decr on neck side.

Row 36 Work 3 cl patt, 5 tc htr (working of tricot half treble: yoh, insert hook into next f b, yoh, draw through f b, yoh, draw through 2 lp leaving rem lp on hook), then tc dc to end.

L ch: Through 2.

LEFT FRONT

Make 55 ch.

Row 1 T foundation row.

Row 2 2 ch, 1 T, 1 cl, cont patt to last 10 f b, 1 T into each of last 10 f b for button-band.

Rows 3 to 12 As row 2.

Rows 13 to 25 Work as rows 13 to 25 of right front with the 10 T band on the left hand side.

Row 26 Armhole shaping: 1 sl st into each of next 6 f b, 2 ch, cont in patt.

Rows 27 to 28 1 decr T at right hand side.

Rows 29 to 32 Work straight in patt.

Row 33 12 tc dc at end.

L ch: Once through 1, 11 times through 2, 2 ch, through 2 to end.

Rows 34 to 35 1 decr T on the neck side.

Row 36 4 tc dc, 5 tc htr, cont patt, cast off with l ch through 2.

SLEEVES

Make 47 ch.

Row 1 T foundation row.

Rows 2 to 5 Work straight in cl patt.

Row 6 1 incr T (2 T into 1 f b) on each side. Then inc on rows 9 and 12, cont straight to row 18.

Row 19 Armhole shaping: 1 sl st to

each of next 4 f b, 2 ch, patt to last 5 f b, 1 tc dc into each of last 5 f b.

L ch: Once through 1, 4 times through 2, 2 ch, through 2 to end.

Rows 20 to 25 1 decr T at each side.

L ch: Through 2 to end for each row.

Row 26 1 decr T at each side. Cast off with L ch through 3.

FINISHING AND COLLAR

Sew seams together with flat seam.

Buttonholes are made by stitching around 5th and 6th treble of the buttonhole-band in rows 10, 15, 20 and 25.

Collar Worked with the inside of garment facing. Miss 5 T each side, work in between 3 treble rows for collar and 3 rows of tc dc right around the collar for a neat finish. Sew on buttons.
Lining of a suitable material may be sewn inside if required.

Colour illustration opp. p. 87.

MORE CLUSTER PATTERNS

1. Cluster Pattern

Worked over an uneven number of ch.

Make 21 ch.

Row 1 Yoh, insert hook into 5th ch from hook, * yoh, draw through ch, yoh, draw through 2 lp, yoh, insert hook into next ch, yoh, draw through ch, (yoh, draw through 2 lp) twice, yoh, draw through 1 lp

leaving rem lp on hook * (1 cluster made), yoh, insert hook into next ch, work 1 cl as from * to * into the 2 ch and into every ch pair to last ch, 1 T into last ch.
L ch: (Through 1, through 2) to end.
Row 2 3 ch, 1 T into 1st ch sp looping also under the connecting bar between the clusters, 1 cl into each ch sp and under connecting bar to last ch sp, 1 T into last ch sp, 1 T into last f b.
L ch: Through (2-1-2-1) to last 2 T, once through 1, once through 3.
Row 3 3 ch, * 1 cl into next ch sp looping under connecting bar between clusters, rep from * to end, 1 T into last f b.
L ch: Through (1-2-1-2) to end.
Row 4 As row 2.
Row 5 As row 3.

(This cluster is illustrated with the following cluster increase pattern.)

2. Cluster Increase
This pattern is useful for the making of a flared skirt. Worked over an uneven number of ch.

Make 37 ch.
Row 1 Yoh, insert hook into 5th ch, 1 cl (yoh, draw through ch, yoh, draw through 2 lp leaving rem lp on hook, yoh, insert hook into next ch, yoh, draw through ch, (yoh, draw through 2 lp) twice, yoh, draw through 1 lp (leaving rem lp on hook), work cl into each rem ch pair to end, 1 T into last ch.
L ch: Once through 1, * once through 2, twice through 1, rep from * to last cl, once through 2, once

through 1, once through 2.
Row 2 3 ch, 1 T into 1 ch sp. 1 cl into each of next 4 2 ch sp, 2 cl into next 2 ch sp, 1 cl into each of next 5 2 ch sp, 2 cl into next 2 ch sp, 1 cl into each of next 4 2 ch sp, 1 T into last sp, 1 T into last f b.
L ch: Once through 2, (twice through 1, once through 2) to end.
Row 3 3 ch, 1 cl into each of next 5 ch sp, 2 cl into next 2 ch sp, 1 cl into each of next 6 2 ch sp, 2 cl into next 2 ch sp, 1 cl into each of next 5 2 ch sp, 1 T into last f b.
L ch: As row 1.
Row 4 3 ch, 1 T into 1st ch sp, 1 cl into each of next 5 2 ch sp, 2 cl into next 2 ch sp, 1 cl into each of next 7 2 ch sp, 2 cl into next 2 ch sp, 1 cl into each of next 5 2 ch sp, 1 T into last sp,. 1 T into last f b.
L ch: As row 2.
Row 5 3 ch, 1 cl into each of next 6 2 ch sp, 2 cl into next 2 ch sp, 1 cl into each of next 8 2 ch sp, 2 cl into next 2 ch sp, 1 cl into each of next 6 2 ch sp, 1 T into last f b.
L ch: As row 1.
Row 6 3 ch, 1 T into 1st ch sp, 1 cl into each of next 6 2 ch sp, 2 cl into next 2 ch sp, 1 cl into each of next 9 2 ch sp, 2 cl into next 2 ch sp, 1 cl into each of next 6 2 ch sp, 1 T into next ch sp, 1 T into last f b.
L ch: As row 2.
Row 7 3 ch, 1 cl into each of next 7 2 ch sp, 2 cl into next 2 ch sp, 1 cl into each of next 10 2 ch sp, 2 cl into next 2 ch sp, 1 cl into

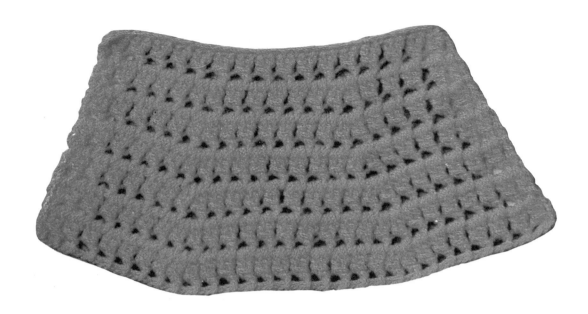

each of next 7 2 ch sp, 1 T into last f b.
L ch: As row 1.

The piece resembles one half of a skirt. Sewn together, it could be used as the skirt for a small doll, or two such pieces joined would make a skirt for a larger doll.

With some skill and experience you should be able to make a skirt for yourself by adapting this pattern to your size!

3. Cluster Lace

Worked over a ch multiple of 8 with a fine (5 or 6 ply) wool.

Make 40 ch.
Row 1 1 T into 4th ch from hook, * miss 2 ch, 1 T into each of next 2 ch, rep from * to end.
L ch: Through 2, (twice through 1, twice through 2) to end.
Row 2 3 ch, miss 1 f b, 1 cluster into next 2 ch sp worked as follows: 3 DT into ch sp leaving last lp of each DT on hook, yoh, draw through these 3 lp leaving rem lp on hook.
* miss 2 f b, 2 T into next 2 ch sp, miss 2 f b, 1 cl into next 2 ch sp, rep from * to last 2 f b, miss next f b, 1 T into last f b.
L ch: ** Twice through 1, through 2, twice through 1, through 2-1-2, rep from ** to and incl last cl, (twice through 1, once through 2) twice.
Row 3 4 ch, miss next 2 ch, 2 T into next f b, * miss (2 ch, 1 f b), 1 cl into next 1 ch sp as described in row 2, miss (1 f b, 2 ch), 2 T into next f b, rep from * to last 2 ch, miss 2 ch, 1 DT into last f b.
L ch: (Twice through 1, through 2-1-2, twice through 1, through 2) to end.

114

Row 4 3 ch, miss 1 f b, 1 cl into

next 1 ch sp, * miss (1 f b, 2 ch), 2 T into next f b, miss (2 ch, 1 f b), 1 cl into next 1 ch sp, rep from * to and incl last 1 ch sp, miss (1 f b, 2 ch), 1 T into last f b.

L ch: As row 2.
Row 5 As row 3.
Row 6 As row 4.

Note: In any tricot chain space you will notice a connecting yarn between the stitches. When working the stitches in the following row always insert hook under this connecting yarn otherwise the crocheted article will drop.

MORE PATTERNS AND GARMENTS

BUNDLE PATTERN
Worked over a ch of multiple of 4.

Make 40 ch.
Row 1 1 T into 4th ch, 1 T into each ch to end.
L ch: Through 2.
Row 2 2 ch, * miss 1 f b, 1 T into each of next 3 f b, 1 T into missed f b across front of the 3 T, rep from * to last f b, 1 T into last f b.
L ch: Through 2.
Rows 3 to 9 As row 2.
Row 10 2 ch, 1 T into each f b to end.
L ch: Through 2.

A delicate decorative pattern for cardigans, baby jackets and other garments.

SIMPLE SHELL PATTERN
Worked over a multiple of 5 plus 9 ch.

Make 54 ch.
Row 1 1 T into 4th ch, 2 T into next ch, 1 T into next ch, * miss 2 ch, 1 T into next ch, 2 T into next ch, 1 T into next ch, rep from * to last 3 ch, miss 2 ch, 1 T into last ch.
L ch: Twice through 2, (twice through 1, 4 times through 2) to last 3 T, twice through 1, 3 times through 2.
Row 2 2 ch, miss 2 f b, work 4 T into 2 ch sp inserting hook also under connecting bar between T's, * miss 4 f b, 4 T into next 2 ch sp as described above, rep from * to last 3 f b, miss 2 f b, 1 T into last f b.
L ch: As row 1.
Rows 3 to 8 As row 2.

SHELL PATTERN
Worked over a multiple of 7 plus 3 ch.

Make 31 ch.
Row 1 1 T into 4th ch, 1 T into next ch, * miss 2 ch, 1 T into each of next 5 ch, rep from * to last 4 ch, miss 2 ch, 1 T into each of last 3 ch.
L ch: Twice through 2 (twice through 1, 5 times through 2), to last 3 T, twice through 1, 3 times through 2.
Row 2 2 ch, miss 2 T, 4 T into 2 ch sp looping also under the connecting bar between T's, * miss 2 T, 1 T into next f b, miss 2 T, 4 T into next 2 ch sp worked as above, rep from * to last 3 T, miss 2 T, 1 T into last f b.
L ch: As row 1.
Rows 3 to 8 As row 2.

This pattern can also be worked with 6 or 8 or even 10 trebles into the one space. Working more trebles into the one space is another way of increasing, such as in the working of an A-line skirt from the waist down.

Shell patterns are particularly suited for skirts, dresses and baby-wear.

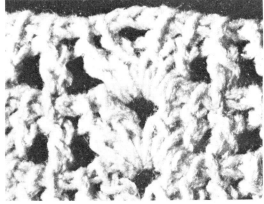

DRESS FOR THE SPRINGTIME

Materials
375 g (13 oz) foundation colour *(A)* — deep blue, purple or red
50 g (2 oz) contrasting colour *(B)* — white or light colour, both in 12 ply wool or acrylic yarn.
Hook 5.00 (no. 6), crochet hook 4.50 (no. 7).
Zip fastener or buttons.

Measurements
To fit 86 cm (34 in) bust, 61 cm (24 in) waist, 89 cm (35 in) hip.
Tension: 7 trebles to 5 cm (2 in), 2 rows to 5 cm (2 in).

SKIRT FRONT
Make 59 ch in *A*.
Row 1 1st T into 4th ch, 1 T into each of next 3 ch, 1 cluster into next 1 ch as follows: (yoh, insert hook into ch, yoh, draw through ch) 3 times (6 lp on hook), yoh, draw through the 6 lp, yoh, draw through 1 lp leaving rem lp on hook. * 1 T into each of next 4 ch, 1 cl into next ch, rep from * to end, 1 T into last ch.
L ch: 3 times through 2, (twice through 1, 5 times through 2) to last 2 T, twice through 1, 3 times through 2.
Row 2 2 ch, miss 2 T, 4 T into next 2 ch sp, * miss 2 T, 1 cl around next cl, miss 2 T, 4 T into 2 ch sp, rep from * to and incl last 2 ch sp, miss 2 T, 1 cl around next cl, 1 T into last. f b.
L ch: As row 1.
Rows 3 to 4 As row 2.
Row 5 2 ch, miss 2 T, 6 T into next 2 ch sp, * miss 2 T, 1 cl around next cl, miss 2 T, 6 T into 2 ch sp, rep from * to incl last 2 ch sp, miss 2 T, 1 cl around next cl, 1 T into last f b.
L ch: 4 times through 2 (3 times through 1, 7 times through 2), to last 4 T, 3 times through 1, 4 times through 2.
Row 6 2 ch, * miss 3 T, 6 T into next 3 ch sp, miss 3 T, 1 cl around next cl, rep from * to last f b, 1 T

into last f b.
L ch: As row 5.
Rows 7 to 11 As row 6 with row 10 in *B* colour, others in *A*.

Row 12 2 ch, * miss 3 T, 8 T into next 3 ch sp, miss 3 T, 1 cl around next cl, rep from * to end, 1 T into last f b.
L ch: 5 times through 2, (3 times through 1, 9 times through 2) to last 5 T 3 times through 1, 5 times through 2.
Row 13 2 ch, * miss 4 T, 8 T into 3 ch sp, miss 4 T, 1 cl around next cl, rep from * to end, 1 T into last f b.
L ch: As row 12.
Rows 14 to 18 As row 13 with last row in *B*. Fasten off.

SKIRT BACK
Work same as skirt front.

BODICE FRONT
Row 1 Insert hook into the right side corner of skirt front, draw yarn through, 2 ch, 1 T into each foundation ch of skirt front (57 T).
L ch: Through 2 to end.
Row 2 2 ch, * insert hook into next 2 f b for 1 T, rep from * to end.
L ch: (Through 1, through 2) to end.

Row 3 2 ch, 1 T into each f b to end.
L ch: As row 2.
Rows 4 to 5 As row 3.
Row 6 2 ch, 1 T into each of next 7 f b, 2 T into next f b, 1 T into each of next 11 f b, 2 T into next f b, 1 T into each of next 8 f b.
L ch: As row 2.

Row 7 2 ch, 1 T into each f b to end.
L ch: As row 2.
Row 8 2 ch, 1 T into each of next 7 f b, 2 T into next f b, 1 T into each of next 13 f b, 2 T into next f b, 1 T into each of next 8 f b.
L ch: As row 2.
Row 9 2 ch, 1 T into each f b to end.
L ch: As row 2.
Rows 10 to 11 As row 9.

Row 12 Armhole shaping (right side):
* work 1 dc with the tricot hook into next ch sp, 1 dc into upper lp of next T, rep from * twice, 2 ch, 1 T into each of next 8 f b.
L ch: (Through 1, through 2) to end.
Row 13 2 ch, miss 1 f b, 1 T into each of next 5 f b, insert hook through last 2 f b for 1 T.
L ch: As row 12.
Row 14 2 ch, miss 1 f b, 1 T into each of next 3 f b, insert hook through last 2 f b for 1 T.
L ch: As row 12.
Row 15 2 ch, 1 T into each of next 3 f b.
L ch: (Through 1, through 2) to end.
Rows 16 to 20 As row 15.
Fasten off.
Armhole shaping — left side:
Count to the 12th T from the left hand side of work, insert hook into the top lp of the 12th T, draw yarn through, 2 ch, 1 T into each of next 8 f b, miss last 3 T.
L ch: (Through 2, through 1) to last T before beg ch, once through 3.
Rows 13 to 20 As right shoulder reversing shapings.

Dress for the springtime (p. 117) with detail of skirt contrast band.

BODICE BACK

Work as bodice front up to and incl row 11.

Row 12 * 1 dc into next ch sp, 1 dc into upper lp of next T, rep from * twice, 2 ch, 1 T into each f b to last rem 4 T, ** 1 tc dc into next ch sp, 1 tc dc into next f b, rep from ** 3 times.

L ch: 7 times through 2, 2 ch, through 2, (through 1, through 2) to last 2 T, twice through 2.

Row 13 Right shoulder: 2 ch, 1 T into each of next 9 f b.

L ch: (Through 2, through 1) to last rem 2 T, once through 3.

Row 14 2 ch, 1 T into each of next 7 f b.

L ch: (Through 2, through 1) to last 2 T, once through 3.

Row 15 2 ch, 1 T into each of next 5 f b.

L ch: Through 2, (through 1, through 2) to end.

Row 16 2 ch, 1 T into each of next 4 f b.

L ch: Through 2, (through 1, through 2) to end.

Rows 17 to 20 2 ch, 1 T into each of next 3 f b.

L ch: (Through 2, through 1) to end.

Left shoulder

Row 13 Count 10 f b from left armhole shaping towards the centre, insert hook into 10th f b, 2 ch, 1 T into each of next 9 f b.

L ch: (Through 2, through 1) to last 2 T, once through 3.

Row 14 2 ch, 1 T into each of next 7 f b.

L ch: (Through 2, through 1) to last 2 T, once through 3.

Row 15 2 ch, 1 T into each of next 5 f b.

L ch: Through 1, (through 2, through 1) to last 2 T, once through 3.

Row 16 2 ch, 1 T into each of next 4 f b.

L ch: Through 1-2-1-2-1-3.

Rows 17 to 20 2 ch, 1 T into each of next 3 f b.

L ch: (Through 1, through 2) to end. Fasten off.

FINISHING

With the *A* coloured yarn sew garment together with flat seams leaving 18 to 20 cm (7-8 in) open on the left side of the waist for zip fastener or buttons, whichever you prefer. Leave the shoulders open.

Left armhole edging

With the crocheting hook and still in main *A* colour work 1 row of dc around armhole starting at the back shoulder left side to the top front. Fasten off.

With the tricot hook again and in colour *B* starting again at the back shoulder work a tricot edge into the dc row as follows: 1 lp through 1st dc, * yoh, insert hook into next dc, yoh, draw through dc, rep from * leaving all loops on hook. L ch: Once through 2, then through 3 to end.

Right armhole edging

Starting at the right shoulder front work 1 row of dc in main colour *A* around armhole to the back, then with contrast colour *B* work tricot

Dress with frill (p. 122).

edge the same way as for the left side.

Neck opening
Join right shoulder seam.
Starting on the left shoulder edge work 1 row of dc around opening in *A*. With tricot hook and *B* colour work tricot edge as for armholes starting at the top of the left shoulder.
Join left shoulder seam.

Belt
Sew in zip fastener or buttons and button-loops. Make 160 ch in *B* colour for a belt, work sl st into each ch, fasten off. Fit in belt into spaces at waist.
Colour illustration opp. p. 118.

TREBLE AND TRICOT KNIT STITCH COMBINATION
Worked over a multiple of 7 plus 1 ch.

Make 50 ch.
Row 1 1 T into 4th ch, miss 1 ch, 1 T into each of next 2 ch, * miss 2 ch, 1 T into each of next 2 ch, miss 1 ch, 1 T into each of next 2 ch, rep from * to last ch, 1 T into last ch.
L ch: Twice through 2, twice through 1, twice through 2, (through 1-2-2-1-1-2-2-) to end.
Row 2 2 ch, * miss 2 T, 4 T into next 2 ch sp looping also under connecting bar, miss 2 T, 1 K into next 1 ch sp (work knit stitch as: insert hook into sp and under connecting bar, yoh, draw through sp, yoh, draw through lp on hook), rep

from * to last 3 f b, miss 2 f b, 1 T into last f b.
L ch: Twice through 2, twice through 1, (5 times through 2, twice through 1) to last 3 T, 3 times through 2.
Row 3 2 ch, miss 2 T, 4 T into next 2 ch sp, * miss (2 T, 1 K, 2 T), 4 T into next 2 ch sp, rep from * to last 3 f b, miss 2 f b, 1 T into last f b.
L ch: Twice through 2, (through 1-1-2-2-1-2-2-) to last 3 T, 3 times through 2.
Row 4 As row 2.
Row 5 As row 3.
Row 6 As row 2.

SHELL AND "V" PATTERN
Worked over a multiple of 4 plus 2 ch.

Make 42 ch.
Row 1 2 T into 4th ch from hook, * miss 3 ch, 2 T into next ch, rep from * to last 2 ch, miss 1 ch, 1 T into last ch.
L ch: Once through 2, (through 1-1-2-2-), last once through 2.
Row 2 2 ch, 4 T into 2 ch sp looping under connecting bar between

T's, * miss 2 T, 4 T into next 2 ch
sp, rep from * to end, 1 T into
last f b.
L ch: Through 2 to end.

Row 3 2 ch, 1 T into sp between
beg ch and 1st T of prev row
looping also under the connecting
bar between T's, 2 T into space
between 1st and 2nd 4-T groups,
2 T into each sp between 4-T gr to
last 4-T gr, 2 T between last 4-T
gr and last T, 1 T into last f b.
L ch: Once through 2, (through
1-1-2-2-) to last 2 T, twice through
1, once through 2.

Row 4 2 ch, 2 T into 1st ch sp,
* miss 2 T, 4 T into next 2 ch sp,
rep from * to last ch sp, 2 T into
last ch sp, 1 T into last f b.
L ch: Through 2 to end.

Row 5 2 ch, miss 2 T, 2 T into sp
after 3rd T, 2 T into each sp
between 4-T gr, 1 T into last f b.
L ch: Once through 2, (through
1-1-2-2-) to end, last in row through
2.

Row 6 As row 2.
Row 7 As row 3.
Row 8 As row 4.
Row 9 As row 5.
Row 10 As row 2.

SCALLOP PATTERN
Worked over a multiple of 9 plus
3 ch.

Make 39 ch.
Row 1 1 T into 4th ch, 1 T into
each of next 2 ch, 1 T into same
ch, 1 T into each of next 3 ch,
* miss 2 ch, 1 T into each of next
4 ch, 1 T into same ch, 1 T into
each of next 3 ch, rep from * to
last 3 ch, miss 2 ch, 1 T into last
ch.
L ch: Through 2-2-2-2-1-1, (through
2-2-2-3-2-2-2-1-1-) to last 4 T, 4
times through 2.

Row 2 2 ch, miss 1 f b, 1 T into
each of next 2 f b, 2 T into 2 ch
sp inserting hook also under
connecting bar between T's, * 1 T
into each of next 3 f b, miss 2 f b,
1 T into each of next 3 f b, 2 T
into next 2 ch sp inserting hook
under connecting bar as before, rep
from * to last 5 T, 1 T into each
of next 3 f b, miss 1 f b, 1 T into
last f b.
L ch: As row 1.
Rows 3 to 5 As row 2.

A pattern somewhat similar to crochet scallops; it may be worked into many types of garments, such as top coats and decorative items. It is particularly attractive if worked into stripes of different coloured rows.

STRIPE PATTERN
Worked over an even no. of ch.

Make 20 ch.
Row 1 1 T into 4th ch, 1 T into each ch to end.
L ch: Through 2.
Row 2 2 ch, * loop through next 2 f b, for 1 T, rep from * to end, 1 T into last f b.
L ch: (Through 1, through 2) to end.
Row 3 2 ch, 1 T into next f b, * 1 T into ch sp, 1 T into next f b, rep from * to end (18 T).
L ch: Through 2.
Row 4 As row 2.
Row 5 As row 3.
Row 6 As row 2.
Row 7 As row 3.

This pattern may be used for many garments, such as sleeveless top coats, dresses, cardigans, children's and baby-wear; it can be worked well in fine yarns.

122

DRESS WITH FRILL

Materials
450 (500, 550) g (16, 18, 20 oz) light coloured 8 ply wool or acrylic yarn.
Hook tricot hook 3.50 (no. 9), crochet hook 3.50 (no. 9).

Measurements
To fit:
81 (86, 92) cm (32, 34, 36 in) bust,
61 (61/66) (66) cm
(24, 24/26, 26 in) waist,
81 (86, 92) cm (32, 34, 36 in) hip.
Tension: 10 T to 5 cm (2 in);
14 rows to 20.5 cm (8 in).

FRONT
Make a ch of 74 (84, 94).
Row 1 1 T into 4th ch, 1 T into each ch to end. 72 (82 , 92) T.
L ch: Through 2.
Row 2 2 ch, 1 T into each f b to end.
L ch: Through 2.
Row 3 As row 2.
Row 4 2 ch, 1 T into next 2 f b, 1 T into every 2 f b , 1 T into last f b.
L ch: (Through 2, through 1) to last 2 T , twice through 2 .
Row 5 2 ch, 1 T into upper lp of 2nd T in prev row, 1 T into sp around L ch, work T to end alternating into upper loops and into sp around l ch. 72 (82, 92) T.
L ch: Through 2.
Rows 6 to 47 As rows 4 and 5 alternating.
Row 48 Armhole shaping.
1 dc into upper lp of each of next 7 T (with tricot hook), 2 ch, 1 T into

upper lp of next T, 1 T into next 2 f b,
1 T into each next 2 f b to rem 9 T,
1 T into 9th last upper lp, , 1 tc dc
into upper lp of each last 8 T.
L ch: 7 times through 2, 2 ch,
(through 2, through 1) to last 2 T,
once through 3.

Row 49 2 ch, * 1 T into next sp,
1 T into next upper lp, rep from *
to the centre only for V neck
shaping. 29 (34, 39) T.
L ch: Through 2 to last in row,
once through 3 for decr.

Row 50 2 ch, 1 T into 2 f b to
end.
L ch: (Through 2, through 1) to last
1 T and beg ch, once through 3
for decr.

Row 51 2 ch, * 1 T into next sp,
1 T into upper lp, rep from. * to
last 2 lp, 1 T into last 2 upper lp
for decr.
L ch: Through 2.

Row 52 As row 50.

Row 53 2 ch, (1 T into next sp,
1 T into next lp) to end.
L ch: Through 2.

Row 54 2 ch (1 T into next 2 f b),
rep to last f b, 1 T into same.
L ch: Through 1, then through (2-1)
to last, twice through 2.

Rows 55 2 ch,(1 T into next lp, 1 T
into next sp) to end.
L ch: Through 2, 19 (20, 21) st rem.

Row 56 to 60 Work straight in patt.

Shoulder shape: * 1 tc dc into
next sp, 1 tc dc into next lp, rep
from * 4 times, (1 T into next sp,
1 T into next lp) to end.
L ch: Through 2.
Fasten off.

Right side.
Row 49
Insert hook into sp between T's at
centre, 2 ch, * 1 T into upper lp of
next T, 1 T into next sp, rep from
* to end. 29 (34, 39) T.
L ch: Through 2, last in row once
Through 3 for V neck decr.

Row 50 2 ch, 1 T into each
2 f b to end.
L ch: Through (1-2) at last, once
through 3 for decr.

Row 51 2 ch,(1 T into upper lp of
next T, 1 T into next sp) to end.
L ch: Through 2, last once through 3.

Row 52 As row 50

Row 53 2 ch, miss 2 f b, * 1 T
into sp, 1 T into next lp, rep
from * to last, last T into 2 f b.
L ch: Through 2, last once
through 3.

Row 54 2 ch, 1 T into next 2 f b
to last f b, 1 T into last f b.
L ch: Through (1 – 2), last in row
through 3.

Row 55 2 ch,(1 T into next lp, 1 T
into sp) to end, 19 (20, 21) st.
L ch: Through 2, last through 3.

Rows 56 to 60 Work straight in patt.

Shoulder shape: 2 ch, 7 T into upper
lps and spaces, 1 tc dc into each
upper lp and sp to end.
L ch: Through 2. Cast off.

BACK
Work as for front up to and incl
row 48 armhole shaping.
Rows 49 to 52 Work in patt decr
1 T each end of every row as front.
L ch: Through 2 to last, once
through 3.

Rows 53 to 58 Work straight in patt without decr.

Row 59 Shoulder shaping: 2 ch, (1 T into 2 f b) 10 times.
L ch: (Through 1, through 2) to end.

Row 60: Tc dc into each upper lp and into each sp to last 3 T, T into each upper lp and into each sp to end.
L ch: Through 2 to end. Fasten off.

Row 59 Insert hook into f b of 19th and 20th T counted from other armhole, 2 ch, T into each 2 f b to end.
L ch: (Through 1, through 2) to end.

Row 60 2 ch, * 1 T into next sp, 1 T into next upper lp, rep from * 3 times, 1 tc dc into each lp and into each sp to end.
L ch: Through 2. Fasten off.

FINISHING

Crochet the seams together on the inside with dc stitches leaving the shoulders open for armhole edging.

Right armhole — edging: With crochet hook work a row of dc from right shoulder front to right shoulder back. Fasten off.
Start again at right shoulder front with the tricot hook: yoh, lp through 1st dc, (yoh, lp through next dc) to end leaving all rem lp on hook.
L ch: Through 2 once, through 3 to end. Fasten off.

Left armhole — edging: Worked the same way as right armhole from left shoulder back to left shoulder front.

Frill:
Make 134 ch.

124

Row 1 T row with l ch through 2.
Row 2 T's worked into upper lp of T in prev row.
L ch: (Through 2, through 1) to end.
Row 3 T's into upper lp of T in prev row.
L ch: (Through 2-1-1-) to end.
Fasten off.

Crochet the shoulders together on the inside. Sew in all the loose ends of yarn on the inside. Sew the two ends of frill together with a flat seam. Crochet frill onto V neck opening with dc from the right side.

This dress may be lengthened, if desired, by adding extra rows, in multiples of two, between hem edging and armhole shaping rows.

Belt (if required)
160 ch, sl st into each ch, fasten off, fit into sp at the sides.
Colour illustration opp. p. 119.

AN "A" PATTERN
Worked over a multiple of 8 ch.

Make 32 ch.
Row 1 1 T into 4th ch from hook, 1 T into each ch to end (30 T).
L ch: Through 2.
Row 2 2 ch, 1 T into each of next 4 f b, * insert hook into next 2 f b for next 1 T, next T again into 2 f b, 1 T into each of next 4 f b, rep from * to end, 1 T into last f b.
L ch: (Through 2-2-2-2-1-3-1) rep to last 5 T, 5 times through 2.
Row 3 2 ch, 1 T into each of next 4 f b, next T into sp between 5th and 6th T inserting hook also under connecting bar between T's, 1 T

between 7th and 8th T in the same
manner, 1 T into each of next 4 f b,
1 T into sp between 11th and 12th
T, 1 T in sp between 13th and
14th T (both as described above),
1 T into each of next 4 f b, 1 T
in sp between 17th and 18th T, 1 T
in sp between 19th and 20th T the
same way again, 1 T into each of
last 5 f b.
L ch: As row 2.
Rows 4 to 8 As row 3.

This pattern is recommended for
dresses, ladies' suits, scarves, tops
or skirts in 5 or 6 ply material in
one or more colours.

SCARF AND CAP
Something warm and elegant for the
children in the cold season or for
the winter holidays.

Materials
225 g (8 oz) foundation colour *(A)*
and 50 g (2 oz) contrast colour *(B)*
6 ply double crepe wool.
Hook 3.50 (no. 9).

Measurements
Length of scarf: 127 cm (50 in) for
86 rows.
Cap around head: 48 (52) cm
(19, 20½ in).
Tension: 6 T to 2.5 cm (1 in).

SCARF
Make 54 ch (colour *A*).
Row 1 1 T into 4th ch, 1 T into
each ch to end (52 T).
L ch: Through 2 to end.
Row 2 2 ch, 1 T into each of next
3 f b, * loop through next 2 f b
for 1 T, loop through next 2 f b
for next 1 T, 1 T into each of next
4 f b, rep from * to end.
L ch: 3 times through 2, (through
1-3-1-2-2-2-2) to end.
Row 3 2 ch, 1 T into each of next
3 f b, * 1 T into space between
next 2 T looping also under
connecting bar between T's, next. T
into following sp between T's the
same way, 1 T into each of next 4
f b, rep from * to end.
L ch: As row 2.

Rows 4 to 85 As row 3 working rows 6, 8, 10, 12, 20, 22, 65, 67, 75, 77, 79, 81 in *B* colour, others in *A*.
Row 86 2 ch, 1 T into each f b to end.
L ch: Through 2.

CAP
Make 118 (126) ch (*A* colour).
Rows 1 and 2 T rows.
L ch: Through 2 to end.
Row 3 Work in patt as for scarf with 2 T each end instead of 4.
Rows 4 to 16 Cont patt without decr, working rows 4, 6, 8, 16, in *B* colour and all others in *A*.
Row 17 Last row in patt, casting off with the l ch.

Finishing off the cap
Sew together with flat seam joining pattern rows neatly.

Make 150 ch with the combined yarn of the two colours, sew in loose ends. Pull the chain through the holes of the *A* patterns in row 14, pull tightly, make a bow.
Colour illustration opp. p. 134.

COMBINATION "A" AND SHELL PATTERN
The working of this pattern requires some experience in Lace Tricot. When working trebles *into chain space* always loop under the connecting bar between the trebles as well. This will prevent the resulting fabric from dropping in wear.

Worked over a multiple of 12 plus 21 ch.

Make 57 ch.

Row 1 1st T into 5th ch from hook, * miss 1 ch, 1 T into next ch, rep from * twice, 2 T into next ch, 1 T into following ch, ** (miss 1 ch, 1 T into next ch) 5 times, 2 T into next ch, 1 T into following ch, rep from ** to last 8 ch, (miss 1 ch, 1 T into next ch) 4 times.
L ch: Through 1-3-1, then (through 2-2-2-1-1-2-2-2-1-3-1-) to beg ch, once through 2.
Row 2 2 ch, 1 T into sp between beg ch and 1st T (looping also under connecting bar), miss 2 T, 1 T into next ch sp, 1 T into next f b,

* miss 2 T, 4 T into next 2 ch sp,
miss 2 T, 1 T into next f b, 1 T
into next 1 ch sp, miss 2 T, 1 T
into next 1 ch sp, 1 T into next
f b, rep from * to end.
L ch: As row 1.
Rows 3 to 8 As row 2.

ATTRACTIVE LACY PATTERN
Worked over a multiple of 12 plus
6 ch.

Make 30 ch.
Row 1 1st T into 4th ch, 1 T into
each ch to end.
L ch: Through 2.
Row 2 2 ch, 1 T into each of next
3 f b, (1 T into 2 f b) 4 times,
1 T into each of next 4 f b, (1 T
into 2 f b) 4 times, 1 T into each

of next 4 f b.

L ch: 3 times through 2, twice
through 1, twice through 3, twice
through 1, 4 times through 2, twice
through 1, twice through 3, twice
through 1, 4 times through 2.
Row 3 2 ch, 1 T into each of next
3 f b, * 2 T into next 2 ch sp
looping under connecting bar, miss
4 T, 2 T into next 2 ch sp looping
under connecting bar, 1 T into each
of next 4 f b, rep from * to end.
L ch: As row 2.
Rows 4 to 10 As row 3.

MULTI-COLOURED PATTERNS

FAIR ISLE PATTERN 1
Worked in a foundation colour (A) and contrasting colour (B).

Make 72 ch in A.
Row 1 (A) 1 T into 4th ch, 1 T into each ch to end (70 T).
L ch: Through 2.
Row 2 2 ch in A, 1 T into each of next 2 f b in B, * 1 T into next f b in A, 1 T into each of next 2 f b in B, rep from * to last T, 1 T into last f b in A.
L ch: Through 2 to end locking T's in A colour with A yarn and T's in B colour with B yarn.
Row 3 2 ch and 3 T in A, 2 T in B *4 T in A 2 T in B, 1 T in A, 2 T in B rep from * to last 10 T 4 T in A, 2 T in B. 1 T in A
L ch: As row 2.
Row 4 (A) 2 ch, 1 T into each f b to end.
L ch: Through 2.
Colour illustration opp. p. 134.

FAIR ISLE PATTERN 2
This simple practice piece demonstrates the possibilities of combining colours and using different stitches within the one article. Worked in main colour (A) and contrasting colour (B).

Make 50 ch in A.
Row 1 (A) 1 T into 4th ch, 1 T into each ch to end.
L ch: Through 2.
Row 2 2 ch in A, 2 T in A, * 6 T in B, 3 T in A, rep from * to end.
L ch: Through 2, locking A with A and B with B.
Row 3 2 ch in A, 4 T in A, * 2 T in B, 7 T in A, rep from * to last 7 T, 2 T in B, 5 T in A.
L ch: As row 2.
Row 4 Tc dc row in B.
Row 5 Tc dc row in A.
Row 6 Tc dc row in B.
Row 7 As row 3.
Row 8 As row 2.
Row 9 T row in A.
Colour illustration opp. p. 134.

DIAMOND FAIR ISLE
In colours A and B.

Make 42 ch in A.
Row 1 1 T into 4th ch, 1 T into each ch to end.
L ch: Through 2.
Row 2 2 ch, join in B, miss 1 f b, 1 T into next f b, 1 T into missed f b (crossed treble, cr T, completed), 1 T into each of next 10 f b in A, cr T in B, 1 T into each of next 10 f b in A, 1 cr T in B, 1 T into each of next 10 T in A, 1 cr T in B, 1 T into last f b in A.
L ch: Through 2 to end locking A coloured T's with A yarn and contrasting coloured B T's with B yarn.
Row 3 2 ch in A, 1 cr T in B, 8 T in A, 1 cr T in B, 2 T in A, 1 cr T in B, 6 T in A, 1 cr T in B, 2 T in A, 1 cr T in B, 8 T in A, 1 cr T in B, last T in A.
L ch: As row 2.
Work beg ch and T into f b in A and all cr T in B:

Row 4 2 ch, 1 cr T, 6 T, 1 cr T, 6 T, 1 cr T, 2 T, 1 cr T, 6 T, 1 cr T, 6 T, 1 cr T, 1 T.
L ch: As row 2.
Row 5 2 ch, 1 cr T, 4 T, 1 cr T, 10 T, 1 cr T, 10 T, 1 cr T, 4 T, 1 cr T, 1 T.
L ch: As row 2.
Row 6 As row 4.
Row 7 As row 3.
Row 8 As row 2.
Row 9 in *A*: 2 ch, 1 T into each f b to end.
L ch: Through 2.

Finishing
Sl st through each f b of prev row; fasten off at the left side of work.
Colour illustration opp. p. 134.

TWO TONE PATTERN
In treble, double treble and tricot plain stitches. Work rows 4, 7, 10 and 13 in contrasting colour, others in main colour.

Make 48 ch.
Row 1 1 T into 4th ch, 1 T into each ch to end.
L ch: Through 2.
Row 2 2 ch, * insert hook into next 2 f b for 1 T, rep from * to end, 1 T into last f b.
L ch: Through 1-1-3, then (through 1-1-1-3-) to beg ch, through 1-1-2 at the end.
Row 3 3 ch, 2 T into next ch sp inserting hook also under connecting bar, * miss 2 T, 3 T into next 3 ch sp, rep from * to end.
L ch: Twice through 2 (through 1-2-2-2-) to end.

Row 4 Join in contrast colour by drawing 1 lp through 1st lp, 1 tc dc into each of next 2 f b, * 1 DT insert hook around the upper part of the 'A' formed by two T in second row , 1 tc dc into each of next 3 f b, rep from * to end.
L ch: Through 2.
Row 5 (main colour) 2 ch, * insert hook into 2 f b for 1 T, rep from * to end, 1 T into last f b.
L ch: As row 2.
Rows 6 to 14 Rep rows 3 to 5.
Colour illustration opp. p. 134.

BUTTONHOLE EXERCISE
Make 13 ch.
Row 1 1 T into 4th ch, 1 T into each ch to end.
L ch: Through 2 to end.
Row 2 2 ch, 1 T into each of next 3 f b, 1 decr T by working 1 T into next 2 f b, 1 T into each of next 5 f b.
L ch: 4 times through 2, once through 1, through 2 to end.
Row 3 2 ch, 1 T into each of next 4 f b, 1 T into the 1 ch sp

connecting bar between the trebles as illustrated, 1 T into each of next 5 f b.

L ch: Through 2 to end.

Row 4 2 ch, 1 T into each f b to end.

L ch: Through 2 to end.

On Finishing

For a neat finish on any tricot or Lace Tricot article: after completing the lock chain of the last row, work slip stitch into each front bar in the last row.

inserting hook also under the

TREBLE-AROUND-TREBLE IN LACE TRICOT

1. Stripe pattern in contrasting colours

Worked over an uneven no of ch in colours A and B.

Make 35 ch in A.
Row 1 (A) 1 T into 4th ch, 1 T into each ch to end.
L ch: Through 2.
Row 2 2 ch (A), * 1 DT around next T in B, 1 T into next f b in A, rep from * to end.
L ch: Through 2 to end locking DT with B yarn and T with A.
Rows 3 to 6 As row 2.

2. Treble-around-treble pattern

Worked over a multiple of 6 plus 5 ch.

Make 29 ch.
Row 1 1 T into 4th ch, 1 T into each ch to end.
L ch: Through 2.
Row 2 2 ch, 1 T into each of next 2 f b, * 1 DT around each of next 3 T, 1 T into each of next 3 f b, rep from * to end.

L ch: Through 2.
Rows 3 to 7 As row 2.

3. Fancy "X" Pattern

Worked over a multiple of 5 plus 4 ch.

Make 34 ch.
Row 1 1 T into 4th ch, 1 T into each ch to end.
L ch: Through 2.
Row 2 2 ch, 1 T into next f b, * miss 2 T, 1 DT around next T, 1 T into 2nd missed f b across back of DT just worked, 1 DT around 1st missed T across front, 1 T into each of next 2 f b, rep from * to end.
L ch: Through 2.

Row 3 2 ch, 1 T into each f b to end.
L ch: Through 2.
Row 4 As row 2.
Row 5 As row 3.
Row 6 As row 2.

This interesting little pattern should waken your fantasy to many beautiful designs: dresses or coats, cushion covers or children's wear — or just a decorative pocket or cuff.

4. Rib pattern

Worked over a multiple of 6 ch.

Make 30 ch.
Row 1 1 T into 4th ch, 1 T into each ch to end.
L ch: Through 2.
Row 2 2 ch, 1 T into each of next 3 f b, * miss 1 T, 1 DT around next T, 1 DT around missed T across front, 1 T into each of next 4 f b, rep from * to end.
L ch: Through 2.
Rows 3 to 5 As row 2.

132

CABLE PATTERNS

CABLE PATTERNS

Working around the body of trebles is a very useful technique and is the only way to work *cable patterns.*

Cables are eminently suitable decorative stitches for all types of winter sports wear and for any garment where a fancy, knitted-like effect is wanted.

TREBLE-AROUND-TREBLE CABLE PATTERN

Worked over a multiple of 8 plus 6 ch.

Make 30 ch.
Row 1 1 T into 4th ch, 1 T into each ch to end.
L ch: Through 2.
Row 2 2 ch, 1 T into each of next 3 f b, * miss 2 T, 1 DT around

each of next 2 T, 1 DT around 1st missed T across front, 1 DT around 2nd missed T across front, 1 T into each of next 4 f b, rep from * to end.
L ch: Through 2.

Row 3 2 ch, 1 T into each of next 3 f b, * 1 DT around each of next

4 DT, 1 T into each of next 4 f b, rep from * to end.
L ch: Through 2.
Row 4 As row 2.
Row 5 As row 3.

PATTERN WITH THREE DIFFERENT CABLES

Make 37 ch.
Row 1 1 T into 4th ch, 1 T into each ch to end.
L ch: Through 2.
Row 2 2 ch, 1 T into each of next 3 f b, miss 2 T, 1 DT around each

of next 2 T, 1 DT around 1st
missed T working behind the 2 DT
just worked (this may seem difficult
at first, but very rewarding!), 1 DT
around 2nd missed T across back,
miss 2 T, 1 DT around each of next
2 T, 1 DT around 1st missed T
working across in front of the last
worked 2 DT, 1 DT around 2nd
missed T across front, 1 T into each
of next 4 f b, miss 2 T, 1 DT
around each of next 2 T, 1 DT
around 1st missed T across front,
1 DT around 2nd missed DT across
front, miss 2 T, 1 DT around each
of next 2 T, 1 DT around 1st missed
T across back, 1 DT across 2nd
missed T across back, 1 T into each
of next 4 f b, miss 2 T, 1 DT
around next T, 1 T into f b of
2nd missed T across back of DT just
worked, 1 LT around 1st missed T
across front, 1 T into each of next
4 f b.
L ch: Through 2.
Row 3 2 ch, 1 T into each of next
3 f b, 1 DT around each of next
8 DT, 1 T into each of next 4 f b,
1 DT around each of next 8 DT,
1 T into each of next 4 f b, miss
(1 DT, 1 T), 1 DT around next LT,
1 T into f b of 2nd missed T
across back, 1 LT around 1st missed
DT across front, 1 T into each of
next 4 f b.
L ch: Through 2.
Row 4 2 ch, 3 T, miss 2 DT, 1 DT
around each of next 2 DT, 1 DT

around 1st missed DT across back,
1 DT around 2nd missed DT across
back, miss 2 DT, 1 DT around each
of next 2 DT, 1 DT around 1st
missed DT across front, 1 DT around
2nd missed DT across front, 4 T,
miss 2 DT, 1 DT around each of
next 2 DT, 1 DT around 1st missed
DT across front, 1 DT around 2nd
missed DT across front, miss 2 DT,
1 DT around each of next 2 DT,
1 DT around 1st missed DT across
back, 1 DT around 2nd missed DT
across back, 4 T, miss (1 DT, 1 T),
1 DT around next LT, 1 T into f b
of 2nd missed T across back, 1 LT
around 1st missed DT across front,
4 T.
L ch: Through 2.
Row 5 As row 3.
Row 6 As row 4.
Row 7 As row 3.
Row 8 As row 4.
Row 9 2 ch, 1 T into each f b
to end.
L ch: Through 2.

a. Diamond fair isle (p. 128). b. Fair isle pattern 1 (p. 128).
c. The attractive pattern used in the lace tricot scarf and cap (p.125).
d. Fair isle pattern 2 (p. 128). e. Two tone pattern (p. 129).

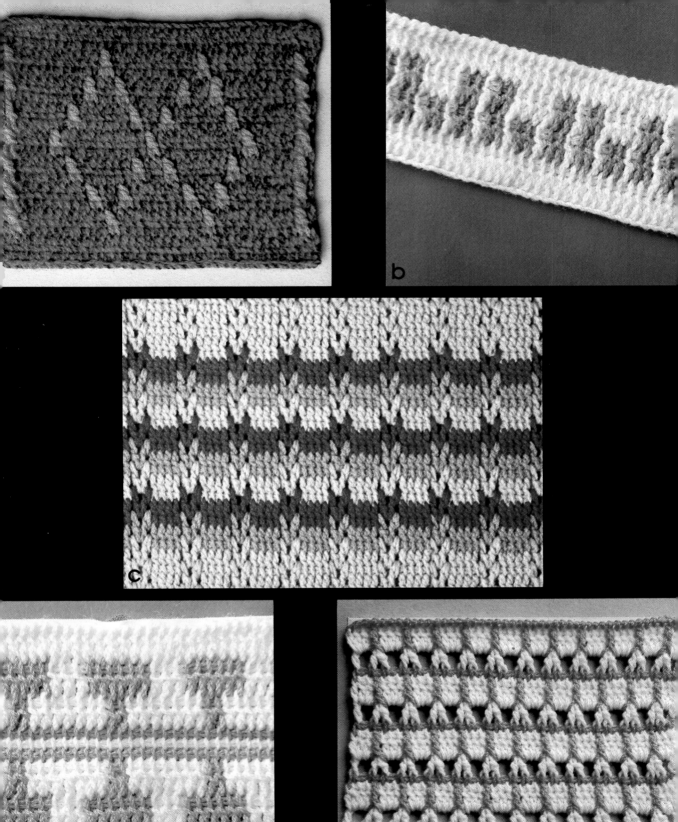

b

c

e

ARAN LACE TRICOT

In this pattern all double trebles around "missed" stitches are worked *across front* of the double treble(s) just worked.

All trebles are worked into "next f b" unless otherwise instructed.

Cross stitch (cr st) or crossed treble: miss 1 f b, 1 T into next f b, 1 T into missed f b.

Make 68 ch.
Row 1 1 T into 4th ch, 1 T into each ch to end.
L ch: Through 2.
Row 2 2 ch, 3 T, miss 2 T, 1 DT around next 2 T, 1 DT around 1st missed T, 1 DT around 2nd missed T, 4 T, (1 T into next 2 f b) twice, 4 T, miss 1 T, 1 DT around next T, 1 DT around missed T, 10 T, 1 cr st, 10 T, miss 1 T, 1 DT around next T, 1 DT around missed T, 4 T, (1 T into next 2 f b) twice, 4 T, miss 2 T, 1 DT around

next 2 T, 1 DT around 1st missed T, 1 DT around 2nd missed T, 4 T.
L ch: 11 times through 2, through 1-3-1, 34 times through 2, through 1-3-1, then through 2 to end.
Row 3 * 2 ch, 3 T, 1 DT around each of next 4 DT, 4 T, 1 T into next 1 ch sp, miss 2 f b, 1 T into next 1 ch sp, 4 T, miss 1 DT, 1 DT around next DT, 1 DT around missed DT * 8 T, 3 cr st, 8 T, ** miss 1 DT, 1 DT around next DT, 1 DT around missed DT, 4 T, 1 T into 1 ch sp, miss 2 f b, 1 T into next 1 ch sp, 4 T, miss 2 DT, 1 DT around each of next 2 DT, 1 DT around 1st missed DT, 1 DT around 2nd missed DT, 4 T.
L ch: As row 2. **
Row 4 2 ch, 3 T, miss 2 DT, 1 DT around each of next 2 DT, 1 DT around 1st missed DT, 1 DT around 2nd missed DT, 4 T, 1 T into 1 ch sp, miss 2 f b, 1 T into next 1 ch sp, 4 T, miss 1 DT, 1 DT around next DT, 1 DT around missed DT,

Ladies' cardigan — aran lace tricot (p. 136).

6 T, 5 cr st, 6 T, miss 1 DT, 1 DT around next DT, 1 DT around missed DT, 4 T, 1 T into 1 ch sp, miss 2 f b, 1 T into next 1 ch sp, 4 T, miss 2 DT, 1 DT around each of next 2 DT, 1 DT around 1st missed DT, 1 DT around 2nd missed DT, 4 T.

L ch: As row 2.

Row 5 Patt as row 3 from * to *, 4 T, 7 cr st, 4 T, cont patt as row 3 ** to **.

Row 6 As row 4.

Row 7 As row 3.

Row 8 2 ch, 4 T, miss 2 DT, 1 DT around each of next 2 DT, 1 DT around 1st missed DT, 1 DT around 2nd missed DT, 4 T, 1 T into 1 ch sp, miss 2 f b, 1 T into next 1 ch sp, 4 T, miss 1 DT, 1 DT around next DT, 1 DT around missed DT, 10 T, 1 cr st, 10 T, miss 1 DT, 1 DT around next DT, 1 DT around missed DT, 4 T, 1 T into 1 ch sp, miss 2 f b, 1 T into next 2 ch sp, 4 T, miss 2 DT, 1 DT around each of next 2 DT, 1 DT around 1st missed DT, 1 DT around 2nd misse DT, 4 T.

L ch: As row 2.

Row 9 Patt as row 3 from * to *; 22 T (no cr st in this row), cont patt as row 3 from ** to **.

LADIES' CARDIGAN — ARAN LACE TRICOT

Materials
725 g (27 oz) 8 ply wool,
10 buttons
Hook 3.50 (no. 9), crochet hook 3.50 (no. 9).

Measurements
96 cm (38 in) chest to fit 92 cm (36 in) bust and 96 cm (38 in) hip.

Tension: 5 T to 2.5 cm (1 in), 3 rows to 5 cm (2 in).

LEFT FRONT
Make 50 ch.

Row 1 1 T into 4th ch, 1 T into each ch to end.

L ch: Through 2.

Row 2 2 ch, 6 T, miss 2 T, 1 DT around each of next 2 T, 1 DT around 1st missed T across front (a f), 1 DT around 2nd missed T a f, 4 T, 3 cr st (cross stitch or crossed treble: miss 1 f b, 1 T into next f b, 1 T into missed f b), 4 T, miss 2 T, 1 DT around next T, 1 T into 2nd missed f b across back (a b), 1 LT around 1st missed T a f, 4 T, miss 2 T, 1 DT around each of next 2 T, 1 DT around 1st missed T a b, 1 DT around 2nd missed T a b, miss 2 T, 1 DT around each of next 2 T, 1 DT around 1st missed T a f, 1 DT around 2nd missed T a f, 4 T, 1 cr st, 2 T.

L ch: Through 2.

Row 3 2 ch, 6 T, 4 DT (each worked around next DT), 2 T, 5 cr st, 2 T, miss (1 DT, 1 T), 1 DT around LT, 1 T into f b of 2nd missed T a b, 1 LT around 1st missed DT a f, 4 T, 8 DT (as before, around DT's), 4 T, 1 cr st, 2 T.

L ch: Through 2.

Row 4 2 ch, 6 T, miss 2 DT, 1 DT around each of next 2 DT, 1 DT around 1st missed DT a f, 1 DT around 2nd missed DT a f, 4 T,

3 cr st, 4 T, miss (1 DT, 1 T), 1 DT around next LT, 1 T into 2nd missed f b a b, 1 LT around 1st missed DT a f, 4 T, miss 2 DT, 1 DT around each of next 2 DT, 1 DT around 1st missed DT a b, 1 DT around 2nd missed DT a b, miss 2 DT, 1 DT around each of next 2 DT, 1 DT around 1st missed DT a f, 1 DT around 2nd missed DT a f, 4 T, 1 cr st, 2 T.
L ch: Through 2.
Rows 5 to 25 Cont patt as rows 3 and 4.
Row 26 Shape Armhole. 6 sl st, 2 ch, 2 T, 1 decr T, 4 T, 3 cr st, 4 T, cont in patt to end.
Rows 27 and 28 Decr 2 T in 3rd, 4th and 5th f b of each row.
Rows 29 to 36 Decr 1 T in 3rd and 4th f b each row.
Row 37 2 ch, 2 T, 1 decr T, 1 T, small cable, 2 T, 1 decr T, 4 DT, miss rem sts.
Rows 38 to 42 Decr 2 T at raglan edge and 1 decr T at neck edge each row. Fasten off.

RIGHT FRONT
Make 50 ch.
Row 1 1 T into 4th ch, 1 T into each ch to end.
L ch: Through 2.
Row 2 2 ch, 1 T, 1 cr st, 4 T, (miss 2 T, 1 DT around each of next 2 T, 1 DT around 1st missed T, 1 DT around 2nd missed T) once worked a f, once worked a b, 4 T, miss 2 T, 1 DT around next T, 1 T into 2nd missed f b a b, 1 LT around 1st missed T a f, 4 T, 3 cr st, 4 T, miss 2 T, 1 DT around each of next 2 T, 1 DT around 1st

missed T a f, 1 DT around 2nd missed T a f, 7 T.
L ch: Through 2.
Row 3 2 ch, 1 T, 1 cr st, 4 T, 8 DT, 4 T, miss (1 DT, 1 T), 1 DT around next LT, 1 T into 2nd missed f b a b, 1 LT around 1st missed DT a f, 2 T, 5 cr st, 2 T, 4 DT, 7 T.
L ch: Through 2.
Row 4 2 ch, 1 T, 1 cr st, 4 T, (miss 2 DT, 1 DT around each of next 2 DT, 1 DT around 1st missed DT, 1 DT around 2nd missed DT) once worked a f, once a b, 4 T, miss (1 DT, 1 T), 1 DT around LT, 1 T into 2nd missed f b a b, 1 LT around 1st missed DT a f, 4 T, 3 cr st, 4 T, miss 2 DT, 1 DT around each of next 2 DT, 1 DT around 1st missed DT a f, 1 DT around 2nd missed DT a f, 7 T.
L ch: Through 2.
Rows 5 to 25 Work in patt as rows 3 and 4.
Row 26 2 ch, patt to last 11 f b, 1 decr T, 3 T, miss last 6 f b.
L ch: Through 2.
Cont in patt as left front reversing all shapings.

BACK
Make 104 ch.
Row 1 1st T into 4th ch, 1 T into each ch to end.
L ch: Through 2.
Row 2 2 ch, 6 T, miss 2 T, 1 DT around each of next 2 T, 1 DT around 1st missed T a f, 1 DT around 2nd missed T a f, 4 T, 3 cr st, 4 T, miss 2 T, 1 DT around next T, 1 T into 2nd missed f b a b, 1 LT around 1st missed T a f,

4 T, miss 2 T, 1 DT around each of
next 2 T, 1 DT around 1st missed T
a b, 1 DT around 2nd missed T a b,
miss 2 T, 1 DT around each of next
2 T, 1 DT around 1st missed T a f,
1 DT around 2nd missed T a f, 8 T,
3 cr st, 8 T, miss 2 T, 1 DT around
each of next 2 T, 1 DT around 1st
missed T a b, 1 DT around 2nd
missed T a b, miss 2 T, 1 DT
around each of next 2 T, 1 DT
around 1st missed T a f, 1 DT
around 2nd missed T a f, 4 T, miss

2 T, 1 DT around next T, 1 T into
2nd missed f b a b, 1 LT around
1st missed T a f, 4 T, 3 cr st, 4 T,
miss 2 T, 1 DT around each of next
2 T, 1 DT around 1st missed T a f,
1 DT around 2nd missed T a f, 7 T.
L ch: Through 2.
Row 3 2 ch, 6 T, 4 DT, 2 T,
5 cr st, 2 T, miss (1 DT, 1 T),
1 DT around LT, 1 T into missed
f b a b, 1 LT around missed DT
a f, 4 T, 8 DT, 6 T, 5 cr st, 6 T,
8 DT, 4 T, small cable as before,
2 T, 5 cr st, 2 T, 4 DT, 7 T.
L ch: Through 2.
Row 4 2 ch, 6 T, miss 2 DT, 1 DT
around each of next 2 DT, 1 DT
around 1st missed DT a f, 1 DT
around 2nd missed DT a f, 4 T,
3 cr st, 4 T, miss (1 DT, 1 T),
1 DT around LT, 1 T into missed
f b a b, 1 LT around missed DT
a f, 4 T, (miss 2 DT, 1 DT around
each of next 2 DT, 1 DT around 1st
missed DT, 1 DT around 2nd missed
DT) once a b, once a f, 8 T, 3 cr
st, 8 T, rep long cable, 4 T, small
cable, 4 T, 3 cr st, 4 T, work last
cable as 1st cable in row, 7 T.
L ch: Through 2.

138

Rows 5 to 25 Work in patt as rows
3 and 4.
Row 26 Armhole Shaping:
1 dc (with tricot hook) into each of
next 6 f b, 2 ch, 2 T, 1 decr T,
cont patt to last 11 f b, 1 decr T,
3 T, miss last 6 f b.
L ch: Through 2.
Rows 27 and 28 Decr 2 T in 3rd,
4th and 5th f b each end of row.
Rows 29 to 37 Decr 1 T in 3rd and
4th f b each end.
Rows 38 to 42 Decr 2 T in 3rd,
4th and 5th f b each end.

SLEEVES

Make 42 ch.
Row 1 1 T into 4th ch, 1 T into
each ch to end.
L ch: Through 2.
Row 2 2 ch, 2 T, 1 cr st, 4 T, miss
2 T, 1 DT around next T, 1 T into
2nd missed f b a b, 1 LT around
1st missed T a f, 4 T, (miss 2 T,
1 DT around each of next 2 T,
1 DT around 1st missed T, 1 DT
around 2nd missed T) once a b, once
a f, 4 T, small cable, 4 T, 1 cr st,
3 T.
L ch: Through 2.
Row 3 2 ch, 1 T, 1 incr T (2 T
into next f b), 1 cr st, 4 T, miss
(1 DT, 1 T) 1 DT around LT, 1 T
into missed f b a b, 1 LT around
missed DT a f, 4 T, 8 DT, 4 T,
small cable, 4 T, 1 cr st, 1 incr T,
2 T.
L ch: Through 2.
Row 4 2 ch, 1 T, 2 cr st, 4 T, patt
to end of last cable, then 4 T,
2 cr st, 2 T.
L ch: Through 2.

Row 5 Work in patt.
Rows 6 to 25 Incr 1 T at each end, working 3 cr st each side on 7th and foll rows.
Rows 26 to 27 Work in patt without incr.
Row 28 7 sl st, 2 ch, patt to last 7 T, miss last 7 f b.
L ch: Through 2.
Rows 29 to 39 Raglan decr: decr 2 T at each side in the 3rd, 4th and 5th and in the 5th, 4th and 3rd last sts of row. Then 1 T decr each end to row 44.
L ch: Through 2.

FINISHING
Sew garment together with flat seam joining pattern rows neatly.

Neck
With the crochet hook work 14 rows dc around the neck evenly decreasing to required size.

Button band
Foundation row Work 109 dc along the left side front with crochet hook.
Rows 2 to 12 Dc rows.

Buttonhole-band
Foundation row Work 109 dc along right front as for button-band.
Rows 2 to 6 Dc rows.
Row 7 1 ch, 3 dc, 3 ch, miss 3 dc, * 8 dc, 3 ch, miss 3 dc, rep from * to last 4 dc, 1 dc into each of last 4 dc, turn.
Row 8 1 ch, 3 dc, 3 dc into 3 ch lp for buttonhole, * 8 dc, 3 dc into 3 ch lp, rep from * to and incl last 3 ch lp, 4 dc, turn.
Rows 9 to 12 Straight dc rows.
Fasten off.

Buttons
Sew on buttons opposite the buttonholes.
Colour illustration opp. p. 135.